CROOKED

CROOKED

A HISTORY OF

CHEATING IN SPORTS

FRAN ZIMNIUCH

Taylor Trade Publishing

Lanham • New York • Boulder • Toronto • Plymouth, UK

Published by Taylor Trade Publishing
An imprint of The Rowman & Littlefield Publishing Group, Inc.
4501 Forbes Boulevard, Suite 200, Lanham, Maryland 20706
www.rlpgtrade.com

Estover Road, Plymouth PL6 7PY, United Kingdom

Distributed by NATIONAL BOOK NETWORK

Library of Congress Cataloging-in-Publication Data

Zimniuch, Fran.
    Crooked : a history of cheating in sports / Fran Zimniuch.
        p. cm.
    Includes bibliographical references and index.
    ISBN-13: 978-1-58979-385-9 (pbk. : alk. paper)
    ISBN-10: 1-58979-385-4 (pbk. : alk. paper)
    ISBN-13: 978-1-58979-419-1 (electronic)
    ISBN-10: 1-58979-419-2 (electronic)
    1. Sports—Moral and ethical aspects. 2. Sportsmanship. I. Title.
    GV706.3.Z56 2009
    174.9796—dc22

                                            2008041646

∞™ The paper used in this publication meets the minimum requirements of American National Standard for Information Sciences—Permanence of Paper for Printed Library Materials, ANSI/NISO Z39.48-1992.

Manufactured in the United States of America.

This is for those who have
earned athletic achievement
honestly.

As well as for those who are trying to
fix the sports world so that
our children and their children
will know the best that sports has to offer.

It is also for my late uncle, Clayton LaMar, who
first encouraged me to write about sports, and for one of the
nicest gentlemen I've ever known who may have been the most
passionate baseball fan I've ever met, the late Roy Forman.

And for my sons, Brent and Kyle.

Other Books by
Fran Zimniuch

Phillies: Where Have You Gone?

Eagles: Where Have You Gone?

Richie Ashburn Remembered

Shortened Seasons:
The Untimely Deaths of Baseball Stars & Journeymen

Going, Going, Gone!
The Art of the Trade in Major League Baseball

Ph-ANTASTIC!
The 2008 World Champion Philadelphia Phillies

CONTENTS

CONTENTS

FOREWORD

MAURY ALLEN

As a kid in Brooklyn who was wild about the Dodgers and then a student at the City College of New York, I dreamed the Impossible Dream.

I would always have the Brooklyn Dodgers to root for (ha, ha) and I would always have the joy, the perfection, and the decency of competitive sports.

The Dodgers moved to Los Angeles (boo on you, Walter O'Malley), and even before that, my standards of moral excellence were shattered by the basketball scandals of 1951.

I was a classmate of Ed Roman, Ed Warner, and Alvin Roth when suddenly they were being led off a railroad train from Philadelphia to New York in handcuffs because they had shaved points. Oh, they didn't dump basketball games; they only took money for staying under the point spread for the benefit of gamblers.

They collected all of a thousand dollars or fifteen hundred or two thousand for helping gamblers beat the system. My alma mater, the CCNY Beavers, never played another game in Madison Square Garden, and college basketball never again achieved those heights in New York City.

CCNY had defeated a school called Bradley Tech of Peoria, Illinois, the previous winter in the NIT championship and the then lightly regarded NCAA for the first and only double college basketball championship ever.

The blow lingers more than half a century later.

The soft underbelly of sports—the cheaters, the phonies, the point shavers, the money grabbers—are examined thoroughly in Fran Zimniuch's book, which reveals that sports is not all romance and purity. It is as much cheating and fraud. It is, to put it more clearly, real life in sweat socks and uniform pants.

As a sportswriter for the last half century and more, I have run into many of these fraudulent situations.

I remember Warren Spahn, the winningest left-hander in baseball history, telling me tales how he ignored the pitching rubber sixty feet, six inches from home plate.

"I don't think I ever threw a pitch when my foot was actually touching the rubber," Spahn once said. "You have to get every edge you can. One of the edges I got was learning how to slide my foot just in front of the rubber so the ball would dance just a little closer to the hitter."

Gil Hodges, Keith Hernandez, and Stan Musial, about as perfect human beings as ever walked these woods, each told me on separate occasions how they moved just a bit closer to a throw from third or short on a close play at first base. Umpires don't watch a baseball sail into a first baseman's glove. They listen for the sound of the horsehide against the leather glove. Bang! The batter is out. Even if the first baseman is a large step or two away from the bag.

I once asked Hodges if he was off the bag when he received Pee Wee Reese's throw from short for the final out for the one and only World Series title by my beloved Bums against the Yankees in 1955.

All I ever got in answer was a wry smile.

There has always been a bending of the rules in sports—ever since the Civil War battlers filled the downtime between battles with some ball-and-bat entertainment that would later evolve into something called baseball.

Athletes come from the general society, and the general society puts a significant percentage of its population behind bars for a variety of sins—from the excessive drinking of a Babe Ruth to the alleged steroid use of a Barry Bonds.

When kids start playing tennis, they call their own balls in and out. When they play for pay, somebody else calls the lines. "You cannot be serious," screamed John McEnroe as a linesman called his shots. Was the official cheating? Would McEnroe have cheated? This is why officials are always on the job in sports. But in the NBA, even sports officials are under a cloud of suspicion.

Every sport has had its moments of tarnish, as Fran clearly spells out here. I remember when Frank Filchock and Merle Hapes were involved in the 1946 betting scandal as members of the New York Giants prior to the 1946 championship game. It made every game suspicious after that.

I am a Baseball Hall of Fame voter, and I constantly get letters requesting admission to the Hall of Fame for 1919 Black Sox star Shoeless Joe Jackson. It ain't going to happen. The blackened White Sox of 1919 threw the World Series to the Reds, five games to three in the old nine-game format. Jackson hit .375, but he was reputed to not even be trying hard. Some guys are just that good.

It would seem that salaries today are so high that it would be absurd to imagine a professional athlete being involved in fixing games. But there are more reasons than money for athletes not to do their very best.

Cheating is probably as much a part of American sports today as hot dogs, soda pop, or beer. It is the idea of the competition, and the element of success, that matters.

Famed football coach Vince Lombardi was quoted as saying, "Winning isn't everything; it is the only thing."

That concept is part of sports in every way, from a Bill Belichick camera spyglass to a Victor Conte oversupply of steroids. It has tarnished almost every sport, from the abusive parents in a Little League game to the seduced athletes in a professional game. And it is all spelled out here, in Fran's study, with facts and failures of honor put on the pages for all to see.

What's really wonderful about sports is that cheaters are almost always exposed. The games march on. Believe it or not, most contests are resolved through honest effort. That's why sport has been around in the United States as long as we all have.

PREFACE

"Cheaters never prosper, cheaters never prosper, cheaters never prosper," is a refrain many of us remember from childhood. But that preschool chant seems like a distant, faraway cry in the reality that is the wide world of sports of today. Gone forever is the naive yet well-meaning mantra that insisted, "It's not whether you win or lose; it's how you play the game that counts."

Sure. We've seen, heard, read about—and surmised more about—dishonesty in sports over the last decade or so than any fan of years ago could ever have imagined. Whether you call it gamesmanship, stretching the rules, or taking advantage of what is there, to a degree, much of our sports world is now influenced by cheating. This is a harsh and rude awakening for generations of sports fans who were spoiled by the likes of a Sandy Koufax, Johnny Unitas, Julius Erving, Jean Beliveau, Edwin Moses, and Dorothy Hamill. How much longer will it take before we see the BALCO logo on a box of Wheaties?

Cheating. It's been around since the beginning of time. A typical dictionary defines cheating as deriving something valuable by the use of deceit or fraud. People cheat in business, politics, marriage, golf scores, income taxes, and countless other life situations. Cheating is a large part of life. It's only natural that it should extend to sports.

Now, before any of us get on a moral soapbox here, let's level the playing field with some honesty. Has anyone ever given you five dollars too much change at the store? Probably—but were you honest, or did you pocket the extra cash? Did you ever pocket a few dollar bills on the floor at a restaurant, or a couple of twenties you found at the mall?

I can remember finding a couple of hundred dollars on the ground in Ocean City, New Jersey, one day a number of years ago. It was rolled up with a rubber band around it, laying on the sidewalk. No name, no wallet, no business card were with it. Nothing to identify the rightful owner. Should I have asked strangers if the money was theirs? I'm sure that would have brought an extremely satisfying solution to my moral dilemma for the first person I asked. "Of course it's mine," he would say with a snicker. "I've been looking all over for this. Thank you so much." Should I have put an ad in the paper? "Found Money: Read All About It. Call To Retrieve Your Dough." That would have resulted in the same mock thanks.

I'm glad to admit that I pocketed the money, bought a nice dinner for my family, and paid a off particularly big phone bill. So my infusion of found money was good for me, for my family, and for the economy in general—and the phone company in particular. Sadly, it was an incredibly unfortunate reality for the people who lost the cash. I'm sure they noticed it was missing at some point during a weeklong vacation and had no idea where to even begin to search for their money.

So we are all guilty to some degree in life to some degree of cheating, at worst, or taking advantage of a situation, at best. But where do you draw the line? What is good fortune and what is dishonesty?

In organized professional or amateur athletics, where fame and the almighty dollar are in the offing, the stakes are a lot higher than they are when someone "forgets" that muffed shot out of the rough that nobody else saw during a weekly round of golf with friends. In sports, a reasonable definition of cheating is violating the rules of a game dishonestly, or subverting the rules to gain an unfair advantage. And there are many, many examples of athletes who pocketed a *lot* more than five dollars dishonestly.

The old adage "It's not whether you win or lose; its how you play the game" has no part in highly visible, conspicuous athletic events. Once fame and the almighty dollar are involved—or the likes of college rankings, positioning for an athletic draft, or Olympic gold enters the picture—it's Katy bar the door. Even the Little League World Series experienced fraud when pitcher Danny Almonte competed when he was over-age. Apparently, cheating sometimes starts at a very young age.

No matter what hollow words we hear in an attempt to refute the truth, at the end of the day, from very early on we are taught by example that unless you get caught, it is fair game to use whatever means necessary to prosper. Cheaters prosper if they don't get caught. You ain't lying, you ain't trying. And even when someone does get caught—which seems to be happening with troubling regularity these days—there is a certain amount of respect in our society given to those who will go over the line and do whatever is necessary to win, because we live in a winner-take-all world. The spoils are for the victors, and Leo Durocher was right: Nice guys finish last.

In today's sports world, much of the concentration and consternation about cheating has centered on the use of illegal steroids and other performance-enhancing drugs by athletes in almost every sport. But this practice is just the latest in a long, dishonest line of athletes trying to gain a competitive edge over their opponents. Truth be told, while extremely effective, the use of steroids and performance-enhancing drugs isn't even very clever. C'mon—for every alleged doper of today's generation, there is a deeper, much more deceitful, inventive, and—yes—clever history of cheating and pushing the envelope in sports. Taking a shot in a butt cheek isn't particularly inventive or clever. It's just a pharmaceutical injection that affects an athlete's physiology and enables him to train harder, bulk up, and develop keener awareness on his chosen field of play so he can perform better. It's like a Three Mile Island shot of tequila. It certainly has been proven to do the trick—but it's terribly mundane and not the least bit cunning.

The use of illegal drugs is dangerous for those who partake, and it also sends a horrendously dangerous message to young athletes. Other types of cheating in sports, while certainly wrong, can be looked at in a different light. It doesn't take much imagination to get injected with some illegal mojo to turn you into something you're not. Any clod can do that. But don't we at least have to admire the ingenuity of someone who goes to the trouble of corking a bat, or learning how to doctor a baseball in ways to make it do unnatural things? Or a football player who douses himself in Wesson Oil to make it harder for the opposing team to tackle him? Or a college athletic director who cranks up the heat in the visiting locker room to exhaust the opposing team before they even take the court? We're a quick-fix society with questionable morals, as evidenced by the previous examples, but I for one have always at least respected those who went over the line with a certain level of panache. Use your brain, not a syringe.

Did the New England Patriots tape the practices of their opponents and illegally film their sideline signage? Sure they did. What an uproar this caused! But at the end of the day, who cares? Other than some half-baked U.S. Senator from Pennsylvania with an insatiable need for publicity, does anyone really think it is such a big deal that it happened and that the commissioner of the National Football League disposed of the tapes following his investigation? Of course not.

Are the Patriots the only team that taped practices and tried to read lips and steal signs from opponents? An educated guess would be no. But let's also be realistic here. Just because a football team might know what is coming doesn't mean that they can stop it. A team needs talent and good coaching to do that.

Stealing signs and trying to gain some insight about what is about to happen is not limited to football. Stealing signs an age-old tradition in baseball. In fact, it is a time-honored art practiced by those who can decode the other team's signals. Interestingly enough, just as many hitters don't want to know what pitch is coming as do want to know in advance. Try hitting a 90 mph fastball with a round bat—even if you know it's coming. Expert coaches and players can watch a third-base coach for two innings and decipher the myriad hand motions he uses to signal from the third-base box. Managers in the dugout are also under close scrutiny when they flash the original sign to the coach at third base, and the skipper's signs are usually not nearly as complicated. In fact, quite often one of the coaches or players standing in close proximity to the manager is actually flashing the signs, while the manager is just a decoy.

Many teams and players have been accused of planting players and team personnel inside outfield scoreboards to steal signs from the opposing catcher and relay the information to the hitter. One team—the Chicago White Sox— actually used a periscope from a submarine to do the trick.

How about Chicago Blackhawks goaltender Tony Esposito, who once sewed mesh between his legs to take away the five-hole? Or fellow netminder Garth Snow, who wore pads that changed the rules of

NHL hockey. And when Bobby Clarke gave a two-handed slash to the Soviets Valeri Kharlamov in the 1972 Summit Series that pitted Canada against Russia, was that intentional injury cheating—or the spoils of war? Where do you draw the line?

Which type of cheating is worse? Where does sportsmanship end and cheating begin? Are there varying degrees of cheating? And what is it, exactly, that makes so many of us so willing to bend the rules of sports—and, to a larger degree, of society?

It's not just the money. In a survey of Olympians, these world-class athletes were asked if they would rather win a gold medal and die within ten years, or go on with a normal life expectancy and not win gold. A stunning 80 percent stated that they'd rather win the gold. This mind-set is a telling backdrop to the time-honored tradition of cheating in sports. It is also a frightening indication of just how serious some of the levels of cheating have become in our society.

It becomes more and more evident each and every day that in the sports world—as well as in our society at large—cheaters often prosper.

ACKNOWLEDGMENTS

It's often difficult to thank and acknowledge those who motivate you to act. We all sit on our duffs watching television or participating in heated discussions, be it about politics, sex, religion, or the most sacred subject of all—sports.

The last few decades have seen a dramatic change on the athletic landscape of the United States—and the world. Athletics used to be a safe haven. If your kids were in danger of getting involved with the "wrong" crowd, or if they doubted the merits of getting a good education, one of the best things you could do was to get them involved in sports. Kids who get involved in sports usually get better grades, learn life's lessons much more quickly, and take better care of their bodies. Historically, athletics has been a vehicle used by many parents to steer their kids away from drug use, but with all the information we've learned about the dangerous use of drugs by so many athletes, it's kind of ironic to think that sports could keep kids away from drugs. It would be nice to get the world back to that place.

From my own personal experience with my two sons, I've seen the merits—and the disadvantages—of kids' involvement in sports. It's a terribly competitive world, even at the early stages, and we've had mixed results. But at the end of the day, involvement in sports is a great way to teach kids lessons that will benefit them throughout life. Sports offer the ultimate example of the right way to do things. In a vacuum, sports teach what is right and what is wrong. Sports teach the correct way to act, the ideals of fair play, obeying the rules, and honesty. But sadly, sports, like life, are seldom played in a vacuum.

But on the level that so many parents have been involved with for generations, the coaches and administrators in the leagues our kids compete in are the cream of the crop. All across the country, men and women spend their workdays trying to earn a living so their families can enjoy whatever their idea of the American Dream is—and then, at the end of all that, they spend countless hours trying to teach their kids—and other parents' kids—the right thing to do.

This book is for all these honest, dedicated, caring people who only want the best for the kids. For the scared parents who desperately need role models for their kids, folks who live their lives in ways that show youngsters what to do and how to act. They are the ones who got me off of the couch to write this book. It seems like when my generation was growing up in the 1960s and 1970s, it was an easier and simpler life. Sure, there was Vietnam, race riots, and the specter of nuclear war, but the differentiation between right and wrong seemed clearer. Life was black and white—right and wrong. It was a simpler time. But still, even then, there were throngs of coaches trying to teach kids the right thing.

Today, while the world in general and the sports world in particular have become as muddled as a cocktail south of the Mason-Dixon Line, the same kind of people are still trying to teach kids the difference between right and wrong. But we all have cable TV and Internet access, and now we can find out about every pimple our sports heroes have on their bodies. And sadly, many of those pimples are an offshoot of their use of steroids and other performance-enhancing drugs.

In this book, I've tried to trace a history of cheating in sports. Some instances were easier than others, as the long history of dishonest deeds can be so involved that a real history is impossible to really capture. But as you read, you'll see a recurring theme emerging countless times in these pages: the idea that there are different "levels" of cheating. It doesn't take a rocket scientist to figure that one out, but such a simple statement also poses an enormous range of questions. Somewhere along the line, some sorts of cheating became acceptable in our society. I suppose it's only natural that this would trickle down to the sports world. And I've tried to pick the brains of countless people from various walks of life to discover where that line is.

One of my goals has been to make the history of cheating—both acceptable and unacceptable—more understandable. Just because a certain behavior has a long history does not make it right. But perhaps we can understand ourselves a little better if we understand why we feel the necessity to cheat. It all comes back to that invisible line between right and wrong.

I've quoted historians, philosophers, coaches, parents, athletes, and numerous other people in these pages in an attempt to try to make some sense of it all. If there is a silver lining to dealing with the troubling subject of cheating, it's that for every high-profile cheater, there are literally thousands of people living their lives out of the spotlight who still work to instill the proper values into our kids—some of which will be tomorrow's athletes.

To everyone who spoke with me and shared their thoughts and beliefs, I offer my thanks. These people spoke about much more than just box scores; they spoke from their hearts and souls about human behavior. While it is true that we're all human, it can sometimes be very difficult to admit this about ourselves. This is a book about humanity and how difficult it is for us, as human beings, to live our lives with a high degree of honesty and integrity. We all try—and we all fall short. But one of the most significant aspects of cheating in sports is the terrible degree to which an athlete can fall.

Who can forget Mark McGwire's fall from grace? He and his son embraced at home plate after he broke Roger Maris's single-season home run record. In the summer of 1998, he and Sammy Sosa were all that was right with sports. Apparently not.

The tears on the beautiful face of the wonderful athlete Marion Jones were real. That she had to leave her two young children to spend time in prison was horrific. Athletes such as McGwire and Jones and the countless others who have had their accomplishments scoffed at also should be able to earn some degree of acceptance as people who made mistakes and tried a little too hard. And many have paid a terrible price. May they rest easy and be forgiven by society, because while they erred seriously, they also were the ones testing the limits of our athletic society. While in many cases, these athletes broke the rules that were in place, there are also countless examples of their teammates and competitors who broke the same rules—and who never got caught. Many of the athletes who got caught up in this doping mess were just trying to keep up with others and stay competitive.

Much of what I've written about in these pages has been light-hearted. After all, throwing a spitball or corking a bat isn't a matter of life or death. But ask Lyle Alzado's loved ones about life and death and steroids. Talk to Taylor Hooton's parents about the trickle-down effect on teenagers of professional athletes' use of steroids.

To all those who took the time to share their ideas and feelings in this book, I offer my heartfelt thanks. Cheating is a difficult subject that can strip off our protective shields. That so many people took the time to talk to me shows that there is hope for sports, and for our society as a whole.

As always, a special word of thanks has to go out to the fine people at Rowman & Littlefield, who always make my collections of words and ideas look and read as well as they possibly can. It is a professional, supportive, and friendly group of people who understand the fragile nature of writers, as well as the need to have some flexibility in their deadline demands. I've never worked with a finer group of book publishers than Rick Rinehart, Meghan Devine, Alden Perkins, and Jehanne Schweitzer. They are, simply, the best.

This is the sixth book I've written, and I'd like to mention a number of athletes—most of whom did not cheat. But of course, some did. Writing from a historical perspective requires one to speak with people who have lived in particular eras and times. But with each book I've written, I've found that people I've been in contact with, who used to play the games I write about, have passed away with a troubling regularity. Of course, I realize that as we all grow older the likelihood of death naturally increases. But in athletics, as in everyday life, it is always shocking when a person dies so far before his or her time.

While I enjoy almost every sport, my one true sports love is baseball. Cheating in baseball is a time-honored tradition that has become an art form over the years. On the baseball field, the catchers are the field generals. They are the center of activity, and each pitch begins with a signal from behind the plate. Being from Philadelphia, I followed the career of a South Philly kid made good. John Marzano went to high school and college in his hometown before becoming a big-league catcher for nearly a decade with Boston and Seattle. Following his playing days, Marzano returned home to Philadelphia to begin a broadcasting career. He was one of my favorite players and sports personalities, and he was a new and refreshing personality on the air. I was a fan who followed his entire career, and I contacted him about participating in this book. We exchanged e-mails and phone messages to set up a time when we could talk, and he was willing and eager to do so.

But before that ever happened, John Marzano died at the obscenely young age of forty-five. His perspective would have been a fantastic addition to this book, and I would have been thrilled to talk with him. His willingness to work with me was almost as happy a possibility to me as his death was a horrible tragedy. So this one's for you, Johnny Marz—the epitome of the best of what sports offers us. Damn, we miss you on Comcast Sportsnet.

Sadly, he is not alone. Over the past six years or so, many other former players I was in various degrees of discussion with have passed away. There was Andy Seminick. And Johnny Klippstein. And Steve Ridzik. And Johnny Callison. And Bill Robinson. And Ken Brett. And Mike Goliat. And Tug McGraw. And Gary Ballman. And Bobby Murcer. And Mickey Vernon. They were all players with various different abilities, but in my mind, they all represented good things and positive role models. Sadly, with time, the list will continue to grow.

This book is for each and every one of them. They took pride in their accomplishments. They did it the right way, and they were worth getting off the couch for. They were role models for us all.

1

CHEATING ATHLETES

Reflecting Society or Infecting Society?

"It becomes cheating when we move across the line and use techniques where there is a consensus that it is wrong or immoral."

—Kirk O. Hanson

What came first: the chicken or the egg? When the discussion surrounds the art of cheating, it was society that began the dishonest trek in history. How far back do our historic ties with cheating lead us? After all, it certainly didn't start with John F. Kennedy and Marilyn Monroe, Bill Clinton and Monica Lewinsky, the New England Patriots, or even the 1919 Chicago White Sox. A good place to start tracing our litany of cheating is the Bible, in Genesis 27, where Jacob and his mother, Rebekah, conspired against his brother Esau to steal a blessing from his father, Isaac. Jacob became an honored and respected man. But he got his start in life by cheating his brother. The mold was made and the die was cast. How could the rest of us possibly help but to walk down the same dishonest path?

Consider some famous quotes. Leo "The Lip" Durocher is known for his well-known quip, "Nice guys finish last." But as we've already seen, the roots of cheating and dishonesty go much deeper than just sports. If you don't believe me, just ask Esau. P. T. Barnum is reported to have once said, "There's a sucker born every minute." And, of course, Leona Helmsley once noted, "Only the little people pay taxes."

1

It has come into vogue for those with political axes to grind to stand on their soapboxes and pontificate that Richard Nixon somehow cheated George McGovern out of the presidency in 1972, forgetting that, Watergate notwithstanding, that election was destined to be one of the most one-sided in the history of the Republic. The same people also forget that Nixon may have been cheated out of the presidency himself in 1960, thanks to the underhanded behind-the-scenes skullduggery done on behalf on JFK in Illinois. Again, which came first: the chicken or the egg?

This was far from the first election with a questionable outcome, however. The presidential election of 1876 may have been the most dishonest in history. We've all read about President Sam Tilden in the history books, haven't we? No? In the presidential election of that year, Democrat Samuel J. Tilden of New York defeated Republican Rutherford B. Hayes in the popular vote, 4,288,546 to 4,034,311— a 51 percent to 47.9 percent advantage. He also garnered 184 electoral votes to Hayes's 165. This was nowhere near as close as the 2000 election; the networks would have called this one before 10 p.m. So why then was poor Sam Tilden never sworn in as president of the United States?

It seems that there were 20 uncounted electoral votes that were in serious dispute. The states in the middle of the electoral imbroglio were Florida, Louisiana, and South Carolina. All the votes were eventually awarded to Hayes after a bitter breach and no doubt in the ultimate cigar-smoke-filled room. Many historians believe that a deal, known as the Compromise of 1877, was struck in which the southern states agreed to support Hayes if the Republicans agreed to withdraw troops from the South, thus ending Reconstruction. Welcome to Washington, Rutherford. Oh, Sam Tilden, we hardly knew ye.

Cheating is everywhere. Let's face it: As long as there is competition, people will have a desire to find shortcuts. This is true in business, in education, in sports, in life. It seems that just about *everyone* cheats to some extent. People cheat at the top of the business food chain, as well as those at the bottom, cheat. Top students cheat in an attempt to help themselves achieve their Manifest Destiny, and average and below average students cheat just to survive. Do these people have a good reason to cheat? Of course they do. Is there any good reason to cheat? Apparently—because the rewards are higher now than ever before. But so are the risks.

"We all try to get an edge in sports and in life, whether it's getting a good education, or working harder, or networking in a way to enrich our ideas," says Kirk O. Hanson, director of the Markkula Center for Applied Ethics, in Santa Clara, California. "You start cheating when you try to get ahead via means that a consensus of opinion has decided are improper. In sports, taking vitamins is all right, but taking steroids is not. In every game and in every life, there are either legal rules, societal rules, or generally accepted moral laws that dictate how to compete."

Hanson continues, "In sports there are norms such as vitamins that are enhancements that I can use. There are so many new drug formulations and methods of enhancement that we have not decided a consensus about. Steroids were not known years ago, and we had not had the dialogue to rule them proper or improper. That has changed.

Kirk O. Hanson. Photo courtesy of the Markkula Center for Applied Ethics.

"It becomes cheating when we move across that line and use techniques where there is a consensus that it is wrong or immoral."

We live in a winner-take-all society where second best just isn't good enough. You don't win silver; you lose gold. Finishing second in a sales contest or being the runner up in the MVP voting doesn't get you a six-figure bonus. Come to think of it—when is the last time any of us urged our kids to work hard in school so they can get straight Bs?

It's clear that we are part of the problem.

"It's all part of our Star Culture," said Hanson. "We have evolved the Star Culture, which has people being rewarded by outsized benefits. Whether it is Tiger Woods's income as opposed to the number-two or number-three golfer, or the salary of a CEO as opposed to the second or third in command, there are outsized rewards for coming in number one. This has led people to do almost anything for that extra edge. The perception is that if I play it straight, I will never come out number one. So I seek every angle to become number one.

"When you talk about a hundredth of a second in a track-and-field event, or half a second in NASCAR, there is an overwhelming temptation to try to get that advantage. This is even true in academic circles. Disparities in salary will lead people even in academia to do things to try to gain an advantage. And people will tie themselves in knots trying to focus on being number one."

The stakes in our society—and in sports—are higher than they've ever been before. Competition is constant, and the bottom line often becomes the bottom line. Whether we're talking about athletes or successful businesspeople, these people have a competitive streak that actually helps them achieve much of their greatness—but that same streak often leads to situations in which right and wrong can be muddied by the ultimate payoff.

"It's all about getting an edge," says Jerrold Casway, a professor of history and chair of the Social Sciences/Teacher Education Division at Howard Community College and author of of *Ed Delahanty in the Emerald Age of Baseball*. "Getting that competitive edge is the key to all sporting competition. Most people get it on sheer ability. But the need to win is so great that people look to any advantage. With the tremendous amount of money out there, it has become a scientific proposition with this whole steroid thing. It's all about becoming quicker, getting stronger, and being more durable. The owners and the commissioner turned their back on it for years. It's the ultimate modern cheating scandal."

But no matter where else in life we see cheating or people trying to get an unfair advantage, doesn't it hurt just a little more when one of our athletes lets us down? If a businessperson or political leader goes down in the flames of dishonesty, more often than not it causes a cynical response from the masses: The bastard deserved it. He becomes the focus of a Top Ten list on late night television.

But when an athlete we root for—or at least respect—is outed as a druggie or a cheater, it hurts a little more. Some of the most motivated, talented, and egotistical people among us are powerful politicians, corporate CEOs, and the like. But from that same gene pool are the people who can hit or throw a 99 mph fastball, or run 100 yards more quickly than most of us could drive it. The vast majority of us aren't capable of being a United States Senator or running a huge corporation, but at some point pretty much all of us have played one sport or another. We can relate to our heroes who toil on their fields of dreams because we've been on those playing fields ourselves. They just had the ability to hit a curveball better than we could.

It turns out that in this day and age—where the ultimate payday outweighs everything else—even our revered athletes are trying to get more for less. As a result, our expectations have been lowered by their cheating. We still enjoy the contests, but deep down in our sports fan's heart of hearts is a troubling doubt: Is the game on the level? Are games being decided by factors we're not even aware of? A pitcher throws a grease ball because he thinks the hitter has corked his bat. And both are on steroids, just trying to keep up with the other. Cheating has undermined the reason we enjoy sports in the first place. That connection we have always enjoyed with our sports heroes is being lost due to their incredible salaries, their increasingly foul attitude toward fans, and the fact that hardly any of *us* need to use human growth hormone before leaving for work in the morning or shoot steroids into our buttocks during our morning coffee break. But on the fields of dreams, the corporate mentality of becoming number one at all costs has pervaded the sports world.

"The more corporate culture demands results in quarterly earnings, the more likely people will take short cuts," writes Phyllis Davis in *E2: Using the Power of Ethics and Etiquette in American Business.*

Multimillion-dollar salaries aren't enough anymore. At some point we've all felt that our favorite athletes were above the fray of such greed and deceit because they play the same child's game that we all played . . . just a whole lot better. But to hear them try to rationalize their own bouts of cheating, be it a corked bat or a needle in the butt, they are still the same as the rest of us. They had to do it because everyone else did it. Young athletes need a boost to get to the big time and big-time athletes need a boost to stay on top. It's an ugly cycle.

"You're talking about athletes making $20 million a year who want to make $40 million a year," says author Maury Allen, who has written more than forty books in his illustrious career. "A certain amount of cheating goes on in every sport. What are steroids and human growth hormones? Look at the Patriots' coach, Bill Belichick, filming a practice. Here is a guy considered to be the greatest genius since Vince Lombardi and they find out he gets some help. Cheating in sports has gone on as long as sports have been played, and always will be. There is a certain percentage of people who cheat. They do it in small ways and in big ways. In baseball, you scuff the ball. The first baseman cheats off the bag. You cheat around second base on a force out. You cheat with corking the bat. There are so many ways to cheat in sports. To me, that hasn't changed in the fifty years I've been covering sports."

There are countless examples of cheating in literally every aspect of life. While it's fair to say that all cheating is wrong, it is also reasonable to agree that there are levels of cheating in society—and, wrong or not, some levels are more acceptable to the masses than others. A consensus of opinion that some acts are wrong or immoral has not been reached. Strange as it seems, we seem to need a consensus of opinion that it's wrong to cheat.

"Cheating is definitely wrong," says Hanson. "The severity of the moral wrong may range from not a big deal to a very big deal. Look at the fight over stealing signs. Can you write down the signs? There are cases in school where, for example, you may inadvertently see an answer on another person's paper. To use it is cheating. But on the other hand, not to use it is almost impossible. You would be penalizing yourself if you don't. If it's one question out of one hundred and it really was an accident, it's different from taking a photo of someone else's paper with your cell phone."

So it seems that some forms of cheating are looked at as simply wrong, while others fall into a gray area. There are specific rules against certain behaviors that are reinforced by the aforementioned consensus of public opinion. These are easy. But what about those gray areas that aren't nearly as easy to define—or where there is a public consensus of admiration or acceptance of such behavior? While it's okay to bend or break some rules, other law breaking is taboo. Or so it seems. Is it any wonder that we flounder at the edge of the moral abyss?

"It's all relative to the time," says Allen, a graduate of City College of New York who was a student there during college basketball's most notable point-shaving scandal, which occurred in 1951. "The City College of New York scandal was very depressing because it punctured the balloon of the last vestige of American morality. What could be more honest and democratic than a sporting event? Turns out they did it to make money. The one excuse we heard from the players was that they never threw any games; it was all about shaving points. You'd get into deep philosophical arguments, which is what we did at City College at a place called Main Hall. The discussion was part of the argument. Was shaving the same as dumping a game? I think that was all an excuse, a rationalization. Saving points is just as dishonest as throwing a game.

"In the view of some, dumping games is outright thievery, but shaving points is not so bad. Well, we either live in a moral society or we don't. You live in a society in which you think there are certain standards you don't violate. I think the bottom line in sports is that a percentage of games are affected by some sort of bending of the rules. Whether that's immoral is for each individual to decide. My own personal opinion is that whenever I found out about a guy doing something immoral, he was never the same person again in my eyes. Pete Rose was a great pal and hero of mine. He did a lot of things playing the game to compensate for what he may have lacked in natural ability. But the gambling went over the line. That's where you said, no matter what happens, he'll never be the same heroic figure he was. He violated the number one rule of the game. And if you bet on the other teams, you did other things too. I'm a Hall of Fame voter, and in my opinion he does not belong there."

In baseball, for generations there have been players, coaches, and managers who are experts at stealing signs from a third-base coach as he flashed them to a hitter and base runners. Is this wrong? It's not against the rules, and, if anything, the ability to steal signs in such a manner is looked at as an art form. Sometimes a player at bat will take a quick peek to see the catcher's signals, or to see if he is setting up for a pitch on the inside or the outside part of the plate. Whether it is considered cheating or not, the players actually police that behavior themselves. If a pitcher sees a batter peeking to see a sign or location from the catcher, chances are that the next pitch will be headed right toward the batter's noggin.

Some advantages are there for the taking, be it through an honest or dishonest effort. Are we in fact living in a "you ain't trying if you ain't lying" society? Are we a moral society, or a collection of people who skirt the edge of morality? It's easy to be moral and pious when we're discussing other people, but our credibility is put to the test when the behavior directly affects us. Almost everyone would agree that many types of cheating are simply wrong. But it is the gray areas that seem to be defining our society.

"Are there forms of cheating that are looked at as tolerable, ethical, or acceptable?" asks Casway. "Some things can be and others are not. There are levels of cheating where there are things that are looked at as being really negative, like tripping somebody. That's not good. That's bad. Or lying. Bill Belichick videotaped games and was getting opponents' signals. Or the New York Giants were actually intercepting conversations from the opposing coach to the quarterback. That's *cheating* cheating. But if you're standing on second base and you pass signs along to the hitter, it isn't cheating as much. Some levels are tolerable and some aren't.

"I think it's in the eye of the beholder. It all depends on the eye of the beholder, or the eye of the person in judgment. If it's your team, you ask, 'Cheating? What cheating?' But if it goes against your team, then it's cheating. How many people were concerned about Mark McGwire when he hit seventy home runs? Baseball had not made it a regulation that you could not take intoxigins. He did not break a law. But he was taking an intoxigen that enhanced his performance.

"It's up to the individual. And who is the beneficiary of the cheating? If the Morgan Murphy system of stealing signs is cheating, and it was cheating, the Philadelphia fans think it wasn't cheating because they were getting an edge. [Morgan Murphy, a reserve catcher for the Phillies was hiding in the scoreboard with a pair of field glasses stealing the opposing team's signs. With the use of a viathrob machine, Murphy could press on electrical switch and the third base coach would feel vibrations under his feet. He could then signal to the batter what pitch was coming.] After all, everybody else does it. That was the edge. Or guys sitting in the stands with binoculars trying to read the lips of catchers and pitchers. That's why Curt Schilling started to put his glove over his mouth."

So who decides in the end what cheating is acceptable and what is not? If certain forms of cheating do not actually cross the line and there is no consensus yet, just where *is* that line, and who ultimately decides which degrees of cheating are allowed? It seems like a generation ago things were more white or black, right or wrong; now much of what was once considered acceptable falls instead in that gray area.

"People generally assume the definition of cheating and the boundaries of what is right and reasonable versus what is not is clear," says Pastor Mike Wicks of the First Presbyterian Church in Sturgis, Michigan. "In some cases this is right. The news business sells a lot of product building people up and tearing them down, sometimes in a cyclical fashion, like a stock returning multiple dividends. So there have to be some clear guidelines within the culture for a reference point, or this cycle would be impossible.

"However, most of the time even the very definition of cheating varies widely. This is in part because we have adopted guidelines for decision making based on what is good for each of us individually. If a person feels oppressed by the government for paying taxes, keeping more than they are supposed to doesn't feel like it's cheating. Heck, it feels like David beating Goliath. If there is a wide, well-paved road in town with a 25 mph speed limit and we are late for an important appointment, we wonder what moron set the limit so low. I once heard a man call on to a radio show and say that it was his right to drive as fast as he could, safely, at any time in any place. Perhaps this was the clearest enunciation of [the sentiment] 'The world revolves around me' that I've heard lately.

"Does the world revolve around me? If so, then it isn't a violation of trust to commit adultery. It is what seemed right at the moment to maximize life's return for me. I think this is the basic question which, if we asked it openly, might keep us from some of the decisions we make which come under the category of cheating."

To get more specific, much has been made of the New England Patriots' history of getting caught taping their opponents' practices or filming coaches giving signals to the players on the field. Knowing what play their opponents are going to run is only a limited advantage to the defense; they still need to have the ability to stop the play.

And a decade or so ago offensive coaches would verbally give the play to be called to a player, who would alternate plays with another player. The technology that allows the plays to be relayed to the quarterback directly through a receiver in his helmet has made that practice obsolete. Perhaps the best way to avert the stealing of signs is to go back to the old practice of using revolving players as messengers who carry the offensive play or the defensive coverage onto the field.

Staying with football: Defensive players look at what are known as keys at the line of scrimmage. A certain player making a specific move at the snap of the ball often indicates what play is coming. Teams have tendencies—things they usually do in certain situations, such as a third down and less than six yards to go. Is using this knowledge cheating, or is it just really good game preparation?

The willingness to turn the other way and accept the attitudes that allow cheating, or a severe bending of the rules, is prevalent in our society. So just where *is* the moral line in the sand?

"That's tough," admits Bob Shelton of Hays High School, who has coached football for more than forty-four years in Buda, Texas. "I think like in baseball, when someone is giving signals and you figure them out, it's not cheating because it's right in front of you. In the old days, they would use field glasses to steal signs from the catcher. I think that was cheating. That crossed the line.

"In football, the defensive coaches signal the plays in from the sidelines. If you can pick up the signals, that's okay. It gives you a tremendous advantage if you know where the ball is going. When Darrell Royal was coach at the University of Texas, he was kind of driven out of coaching because he just got tired of things like Oklahoma watching his practices from buildings that overlooked the field. That crosses the line.

"In Texas now, we have steroid testing on the high school level. You don't know what schools are going to be tested or when. I've never felt that we had a problem with steroids, but sometimes you as a coach are the last one to know. Things like that are pretty prevalent in society, particularly at the professional level. You have parents who think their kids are going to be a college or pro athlete and they don't understand how few are going to go to that next level. Very few have that special ability to go to the next level.

"The intoxication of winning and getting the adulation of so many people is like a narcotic. That is why people do things that enable them to do things at a better level than they could otherwise."

There is another disquieting factor that creeps into our collective psyches when cheating is so prevalent in the day-to-day world. It adversely affects and weakens our trust in the people around us in our lives. It's hard to build business relationships and friendships on one hand when you're both trying to get an unfair advantage at that person's expense on the other.

How many children hear their parents brag about cheating on their taxes, or are told to lie about their age so they can get into a movie or eat at a restaurant at the "under-thirteen" price? It could be argued that in our society, we actually teach our children about the *benefits* of cheating from an early age. So is a little bit of cheating wrong? At what point should our hands be slapped?

"It's just as wrong," says Hanson about a "little bit" of cheating. "The question is: What is the penalty? If you like little cheating, the danger is that it grows into a rationale for big cheating. It reinforces a culture where everybody does it. Part of the American disease is that advancement is equated with happiness. I think we are about to have a wave of discussion nationally that shows that advancement does not equal happiness. A number of studies about happiness have been done which show that happiness isn't advancement. Once you have basic comforts, happiness comes more from integrity than advancement."

This sentiment is echoed by former major-league pitcher Dan Naulty, who admits to using performance-enhancing substances during his baseball career. "Living a very corrupt, immoral life does not promote any happiness," he says. "What I should have done is played the hardest I could and just kept trying to play honestly. To cheat to get what you want is not the way to go about it."

One wonders if cheating is more prevalent now than it was in generations past. Or does it just seem that way because twenty-four-hour news availability brings us a close look at just about every chink in a person's armor?

"Some people think that the attitude toward cheating in sports has changed over the past thirty years," says *San Francisco Chronicle* investigative reporter Lance Williams, who coauthored the book *Game of Shadows* with Mark Fainaru-Wada. "They think that cheating was looked down on in the past more than it is now. The attitude toward cheating alters from sport to sport. Cheating in track and field has different standards than in baseball. Do we as a society condone cheating now more than in the past?

"It's more of an issue of big money in sports, and as a result there is more at stake. It's a difficult topic. As long as there has been baseball, guys have tried to get an edge. Now, thinking about steroids, you have to look at it in that context. To me, it isn't different. In terms of the acceptance, I'm not sure it's a different mind-set. This is a different era and people are more accepting about cheating. But in baseball, there are all kinds of ways to get an edge that are allowed until it's decreed that it messes up the competitive nature of the game. The means of cheating with steroids changes the performance standards, while others might not.

"I totally understand [that] the problem with steroids in baseball is that it does alter the game in ways that we don't want it altered. It gives an unfair advantage to anyone who is cheating as opposed to those who do not."

Athletes compete on many different levels. Those who cross that line and break the rules are gaining an unfair advantage. But competition begets competition in the truest sense, and there are those who have trouble discerning exactly where that line is.

"Cheating is the result of the stress of the competition in any form," says Jennifer DiStefano, student assistance coordinator for Cherry Hill, New Jersey, public schools. "There are also some psychological reasons why people cheat: worries, anxieties, perception. People are just trying to find different ways to succeed. I think the instances of cheating are about the same now, but maybe a little higher because of the media. People are like copycats. It's contagious.

"We do teach our kids to cheat. We send a lot of subliminal messages. Plus, you see more and more on television about cheating with all the talk about steroids and other forms of cheating. You set the moral values for your household. To be a good role model, you have to be willing to not permit cheating in any form. Our kids only know what they see or hear.

"This is serious because now cheating is more popular at a younger age. Kids cheating in school is where it starts. Cheating is learned between the ages of ten and fourteen. Kids are listening to and watching their parents, and they understand. They understand that what their parents are doing may be wrong. The message they get is that it's okay. The degree of cheating can get higher with the combination of what the next piece of the cheating will be. It becomes an addiction. It's like a gateway. Cheating is a form of an addiction, like gambling or a drug. Once you do it, it becomes easier to do it."

We are all guilty of the "do as I say, not as I do" mentality. If we steal money or cheat on our income taxes, we send a message to our children that is loud and clear. But we also send plenty of subliminal messages that are every bit as telling. Cheating is cheating, but a little consistency in the messages we send might make our kids a little more understanding of the issue. It might make us a little more knowledgeable and consistent as well.

"What disappoints me is the number of apologists who go out of their way to defend themselves, like the Barry Bonds of the world," said Don Hooton, whose son, high school pitcher Taylor Hooton, hanged himself after withdrawal from steroid use. "Guys, we've lost total perspective here. Whether it was against the rules or not, it's cheating. Not only that, but this particular behavior is a felony.

"We're sending mixed messages to our kids. No wonder they get involved. A dad can lecture and talk about not cheating and not using drugs. But then he'll take his kid out to a ball game and stand up and give Barry Bonds a standing ovation. What a contradiction here. Is there any reason our children are getting the message that cheating and [using] performance-enhancing drugs are okay? Look at the drugs themselves. We see advertising comparing the muscle-building characteristics of milk to steroids, or a car on steroids. As a society we need to take seventy steps back and look at it. Is there any doubt as to how and why we've arrived at this point with regard to performance-enhancing drugs?"

If parents are teaching their kids that it's okay to cheat, some of the blame—at least on some level—has to rest with corporate America. Big corporations—The Man—just keep ripping us all off. Look at the price of a gallon of gasoline, while oil companies make profits hand over foot. Or heaven forbid you are late with one of your credit card payments; the fine print that none of us ever reads quite often allows the credit card company to continue to charge you late fees in ensuing months. We're constantly getting screwed by The Man, so in our minds it's okay to screw The Man right back.

"I think that cheating is more prevalent today," says Hanson. "I think there is a tolerance for cheating that did not exist in prior years either because of the idea that everybody does it, or because we're getting ripped off anyway and cheating is our way of leveling the playing field. As a result, we are raising a generation of cheaters who take it one step further.

"There is a cultural reality that businesses are much more aggressive toward consumers than they were before. We're getting ripped off, so it's okay to rip them off in return. All the hidden fees in bills cheat us, so the argument is that it makes it proper for us to rip them off whenever we can. I think that more and more companies are doing more disreputable things, skirting the edges of ethical behavior. And we skirt those edges right back."

The argument could be made that the cheating did not begin with the common folk, but it is in fact The Man who started it all. Credit card scams; high taxes, with many people feeling little or no representation in return; huge corporate profits—it's hard not to feel like a lone survivor on a deserted island of honesty.

"Is there more cheating now than ever?" asks Wicks. "Maybe there is. Do some people have a stronger ethical framework than others? Sure. But we have to look more deeply into the place the supports for that framework are sunk. Ideally, our ethics flow out of what we believe about God. But if you are feeling vulnerable and the only way to avoid being hurt in the process is to avoid the truth or not take responsibility for yourself, it's hard to resist."

It only seems natural that this culture of cheating would extend to the world of sports. It starts at a young age—in our children today. The payoff for a young athlete is huge: a college scholarship or draft selection by a professional team. At the low end of the sports food chain, a young jock is trying to earn his place in the sun. Professional athletes are trying to maintain that sunny spot for just one more big contract. At the end of the day, athletes have the same blinding greed that is so present in the business world. Owners, players, and union personnel are all actually acting in concert to promulgate less-than-honest behavior.

And when it involves athletics, the trickle-down effect on our young may be even more harmful than hearing Dad brag about beating the IRS or lying on his résumé to help him get a new, better-paying job. So while cheating athletes have earned their dishonest stripes from societal attitudes as a whole, they are also infecting society in general and young people in particular with the attitude that cheating pays off—that it's worth the risk, because in the end, there is no doubting the fact that cheaters often prosper. Cheating can help you achieve fame, adulation, and wealth. And they are three things that just about all athletes want—not to mention most people living their quiet lives out of the spotlight.

"Sooner or later, guys who cheat get caught," says Allen. "Gaylord Perry got into the Hall of Fame by cheating. He made it into an art form. Now you're always challenged with the morality of it. Should you, as a Hall of Fame voter, vote for a guy who admitted he violated the rules of the game?

"Barry Bonds I think was a great Hall of Fame player. He is as talented as he clearly is even without steroids. But it just sours the environment. They have rules and you have to play by the rules. It's no different than a businessman cheating on expense accounts. What happens in America is you cheat if you can get away with it. A good percentage of people make their careers by cheating. They take it to their graves. I think that sports is no different than general American life; the values are the same. The only difference between athletes and the rest of us is that they have this rare, incredible ability to play a particular sport. The only thing that separates them from us is that athletic skill. There is no more cheating in sports than in general American life.

"I think America changed during the Vietnam War, and we've never recovered from it. The government out-and-out lied to the American people and we bought it. We thought Vietnam was a moral issue like World War II, and it wasn't. From Vietnam on—with the drug culture and the hippie generation and all the things that damaged American morality—is something we've never recovered from. The Iraq war is a total scam. We just never recovered.

"That's why so many of us totally bought the Warren Commission thing. I don't think they were trying to lie about who killed Kennedy. But I think the mission of the Warren Commission was to calm America down. But in effect, they lied."

It's a vicious cycle that has no end in sight. Be it a track star or a baseball player going beyond his or her God-given gifts with the use of steroids, or a pitcher doctoring the baseball, the message is clear. They don't ask how, just how many. But this attitude has a way of trickling down the food chain to the young athletes in their teens—and even younger—who are constantly being hit over the head with cheating, steroids, human growth hormone, and the idea that if you ain't lying, you ain't trying. Watching a professional athlete put his or her long-term well-being on the line is one thing. But when it begins to affect our kids, then the time to act is already past.

One of the great aspects of sports has always been that they can take fans away from the problems and issues they deal with in their day-to-day lives and into a world where all their fantasies can come true. But now we see many of the same issues and disappointments in the real world infecting the sports world as well.

In many ways, those disappointments are even worse when they are in the wide world of sports.

2

THE SHAME OF AMERICA'S GAME

The 1919 Black Sox World Series Fix

"I've loved baseball ever since Arnold Rothstein fixed the
World Series in 1919."

—Hyman Roth in *The Godfather, Part II*

"Regardless of the verdict of juries, no player who throws a
ballgame, no player that undertakes or promises to throw a
ballgame, no player that sits in conference with a bunch of
crooked players and gamblers where the ways and means of
throwing a game are discussed and does not promptly tell his
club about it, will ever play professional baseball."

—Judge Kenesaw Mountain Landis,
the first Commissioner of Major League Baseball

"I am going to meet the greatest umpire of them all—and he
knows I'm innocent."

—Shoeless Joe Jackson

Scandals may come and scandals may go. But when it comes to sports
scandals, it's a pretty safe bet that the Chicago White Sox team that
threw the 1919 World Series to the Cincinnati Reds is not only second to none, but the stuff of legends. Because of the deeds of up
to eight players on that White Sox squad, that year's team has been

unofficially—but universally—renamed the Chicago Black Sox. Sadly, it never had to happen. But a compilation of events and attitudes on that extremely talented ball club made eight of their players culpable in the eyes of some—but most important, the eyes of Commissioner of Baseball Judge Kenesaw Mountain Landis—for the events of that Fall Classic. And the players paid the ultimate high price for their involvement—banishment from the game they loved.

The saga of the Black Sox scandal may be the biggest, most devastating story of its type in the history of the game. But sadly, it was far from the first. For it seems that from nearly the very beginning of America's Game, baseball has always been a Mecca for gamblers looking to make a quick buck. And when gamblers and money abound, temptation follows.

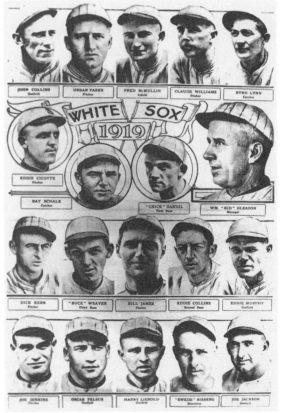

The infamous 1919 Chicago White Sox. © 2008 Chicago White Sox.

It seems much less likely that games would be fixed in today's brave new baseball world, where player salaries have skyrocketed to the point where a utility infielder makes considerably more money in a year than a gambling icon. But that was not nearly the case ninety years ago when the Black Sox traded their baseball souls for a few pieces of silver. And it wasn't the case a generation before that, when the impact of gambling was already being felt by the boys of summer. It has been reported that as early as 1860, a full fifty-nine years before the 1919 Black Sox scandal, gamblers harassed members of the Brooklyn Excelsiors in a game against the Brooklyn Atlantics. The Excelsiors refused to play the game.

"A forerunner of bookmaking, called pool selling, sprung up in conjunction with baseball, and by the 1870s as much as $70,000 might be riding on a single game," wrote Stephen Hall in "Scandals and Controversies," an essay in the third edition of *Total Baseball*, edited by John Thorn and Pete Palmer. "With all the betting, it was inevitable that gamblers would approach players with bribes—even during the 'amateur' era. Players of that era—ill educated, often immigrants—were particularly susceptible; the under-the-table payments they received as amateurs did little to install moral probity.

"Six years after the formation of the amateur National Association, organized baseball confronted its first gambling scandal. On September 28, 1865, the heavily favored New York Mutuals lost to the Brooklyn Eckfords, 28–11. It later developed that two Mutuals players, Ed Duffy and William Wansley, offered money to Mutuals shortstop Thomas Devyr to throw the game. For their role in the conspiracy, which was investigated by the Judicial Committee of the National Association, Duffy and Wansley were banned from match play; the Mutuals, in desperate need of a shortstop, helped to have charges against Devyr dismissed. By 1870, all three players had won reinstatement—a prophetic indication that organized baseball was not yet prepared to take a firm stand against gambling."

A term that came about to describe a game played with the illusion of honesty when the outcome has already been decided is "hippodroming"—arranging a game with a predetermined winner. Such was the case when the Troy Haymakers were accused of hippodroming. One of the team's owners included a renowned New York gambler, John Morrissey, who was more interested in winning bets than winning baseball games. During this time, a Buffalo writer said,

"Any professional base ball club will throw a game if there is money in it. A horse race is a pretty safe thing to speculate on, in comparison with an average ball match."

Another interesting bit of gamesmanship was involved with the 1869 Cincinnati Red Stockings, baseball's first truly professional team. The Red Stockings were on their way to a perfect 65–0 season. Or was it a perfect 65–0 season? A controversial contest against the aforementioned Troy Haymakers ended in a 17–17 tie. This game was clearly an example of gambling's influence on America's Pastime.

Morrissey had reportedly bet $60,000 for Troy to win the game, based largely on their previous game against the Red Stockings, which saw the powerful Cincinnati team beat Troy by a fairly slim margin of 37–31. On August 26, the rematch was all tied up when the first Red Stockings batter came up in the sixth inning and was called "not out" by the umpire, on a call that was not even remotely controversial. At that point, the Troy team, reportedly at the direction of Morrissey, left the field and the game was called a forfeit. Much debate raged over whether Cincinnati's record should be 65–0, or 64–0–1. While the Red Stockings didn't lose that day, neither did John Morrissey, who orchestrated the farce to protect his bankroll. Whether the Haymakers lost is still a matter of debate today.

In August 1877, the league-leading Louisville Grays had a disastrous road trip in which they lost seven games and tied one. Their particularly poor play made many suspicious of their motives. Those suspicions proved correct when one of the players involved confessed to throwing the games, and on October 30, 1877, Jim "Terror" Devlin, George "Gentleman George" Hall, Bill "Butcher" Craver, and Al "Slippery Elm" Nichols were expelled for life. Apparently Nichols had become friendly with a pool seller who paid Devlin and Hall $100 each to throw a game. The Grays were disbanded before the start of the 1878 season.

So while there had been a long history of teams throwing games from time to time, the idea of a group of players joining forces to purposely lose a World Series still seemed far-fetched, although rumors of just such an occurrence were running rampant prior to the start of the Fall Classic in 1919. It was a great time in America. The soldiers were back home from World War I to enjoy the first postwar World Series. On the eve of the Roaring Twenties, baseball was so popular that the championship series was increased to a best-of-nine affair as opposed to the usual best of seven. The tables were set for a great World Series at a great time in history. But what excited baseball fans—and the country—ultimately got that fall was anything but the best.

The White Sox had a fine regular season in 1919, as evidenced by their 88–52 record, which was 3.5 games better than the second-place Cleveland Indians in the American League. But their World Series foes, the Cincinnati Reds, had an even better season in the National League, as evidenced by their 96–44 mark and a 9-game advantage over the second-place New York Giants. But in spite of what had been a very successful season on the field, all was not well in Chicago. For all their wins, the team was very unhappy, to a large degree because the owner of the club, Charles Comiskey, severely underpaid his players and gave them even less respect.

Many have felt that the reason the Black Sox scandal really happened was the cheapness of Comiskey, who most of the players despised. The highest-paid player on the White Sox in 1919 was Eddie Collins, who made $14,500. The only reason he commanded such a salary was that he made sure his salary was written into the contract he'd signed with Philadelphia A's, which had to be honored when it was purchased by Comiskey in 1915. Not surprisingly, he was not one of the players involved in the scandal.

But many of Collins's resentful and jealous White Sox teammates did not earn what could be considered a fair wage. Other players around the league with less ability and who had not enjoyed nearly as much success were being paid twice as much as the best White Sox players. Star performers—such as top-line pitcher Eddie Cicotte, outfielder Joe Jackson, and third baseman Buck Weaver—earned just $6,000 for the year. Outfielder Happy Felsch and infielder Chick Gandil were both paid $4,000 for the season, while infielder Swede Risberg made $3,250. Utility man Fred McMullin was paid $2,750, and up-and-coming young southpaw hurler Lefty Williams earned just $2,600, which rounded out the infamous eight.

Comiskey was able to take advantage of baseball's reserve clause, which literally tied a player to the team with which he originally signed in perpetuity, or until he was traded or released, to keep salaries low. A particularly talented player could hold out and report late to the team in spring training, but Comiskey and his fellow owners ultimately held all the cards as far as finances were concerned. At the end of the day, if a player could not come to an agreement with the owner, it was time for him to get a real job. Not only was Comiskey cheap with his players at contract time, but he often broke promises he made to them. After promising them a big bonus if they won the pennant, he rewarded the players with a case of cheap champagne. The players' resentment of the owner continued to grow exponentially.

Comiskey promised his best pitcher, ace right-hander Cicotte, that if he won thirty games he would receive a $10,000 bonus—big money for someone earning only $6,000 a year. After Cicotte won his twenty-ninth game of the season, Comiskey refused to let him pitch again during the regular season, using the flimsy excuse that he wanted to save him for the World Series. Needless to say, Cicotte was furious, because he felt that Comiskey was just trying to avoid paying the bonus.

Not only were the ChiSox underpaid and underappreciated, but Comiskey also had ridiculous rules that the players resented, such as making them responsible for the upkeep of their uniforms. In addition to the constant struggle because of the resentment over Comiskey, even though the team seemed flawless on the field, it was a splintered group with distant cliques off the field that actually saw players who stood side by side on the ball field literally not speak to one another off the field.

While fans simply saw an outstanding team on the baseball field, they had no knowledge of the unhappiness and dissention in the clubhouse. The team consisted of two cliques, one consisting of Chick Gandil and his seven coconspirators, many of whom were considered easygoing country bumpkins, while Eddie Collins was a native of New York who had attended Columbia University. He was confident and educated, as were his constant cronies on the team, who included catcher Ray Schalk, pitcher Urban "Red" Faber, and rookie Dickie Kerr, all of whom no doubt considered themselves considerably more sophisticated and worldly than the Gandil group, and there was plenty of resentment between those players and the well-paid Collins.

The 1919 White Sox were a talented, splintered, underpaid, and unhappy group of players who were, as fate would have it, ripe for the picking by gambling's seedy elements. While baseball had become a respectable American corporation, it was also considered the largest entertainment industry in the county. And part of that acceptance and popularity led to widespread gambling on the outcome of baseball games. Baseball pools were regularly enjoyed by many. Various weekly pools were wagered on, with bets placed on which team would score the most runs in an inning, or an entire game, as well as which team would have the most wins in a week. Baseball owners accepted the practice because it created more interest in baseball, which in turn greased their pockets and bettered an already burgeoning bottom line. Attendance and interest were at an all-time high, and all was well in the eyes of the owners.

But societal circumstances led to an environment that joined gambling and baseball at the hip. As Eliot Asinof wrote in *Eight Men Out: The Black Sox and the 1919 World Series*, "America's entrance into the World War in 1917 brought about notable changes. When the Government shut down the race tracks for the duration (baseball was permitted to continue), gamblers and bookies who lived by the horses were left in limbo. They needed a place to hang out, some sport to talk about, an outlet for their need to bet. They simply converted their vast machinery of operation from horses to baseball. They applied themselves to doping ball games with the same diligence they'd used in handicapping horses.

"Inevitably this led to tampering with the outcome of games. Artfully, gamblers would find the likely players—preferably pitchers, the key men in any ball game. . . . Gamblers were masters in the use of women and whisky: they seemed to have an endless supply of the choicest of both.

"By 1919, gamblers openly boasted that they could control ball games as readily as they controlled horse races. They even went so far as to put a few choice players on weekly salaries. Exploiting their own talents, bribed players learned to become adept at throwing games. A shortstop might twist his body to make a simple stop seem like a brilliant one, then make his throw a bare split second too late to get the runner. An outfielder might 'short-leg' a chase for a fly ball, then desperately dive for it, only to see it skid by him for extra bases. Such maneuvers were almost impossible for the baseball fan—even for the most sophisticated sportswriter—to detect" (p. 13).

While historians and baseball fans argue to this day over the involvement of Joe Jackson and Buck Weaver, there is no doubt as to the role played in the scandal by Chick Gandil. Gandil had reportedly repeatedly sold tips to gambler Joseph Sullivan—whom he had known for a number of years—about injuries and slumps that might effect the outcome of games, enabling Sullivan to place bets taking advantage of his inside dope.

Three weeks before the start of the 1919 World Series, Gandil met Sullivan at his hotel room in Boston and guaranteed that for $80,000, the White Sox would lose the series to Cincinnati. Gandil then went about recruiting key teammates who could make the fix happen. It was not an easy sell, but as time went on, the idea and reality of this scheme grew as the players met and discussed the opportunity. At the same time, Sullivan was not the only gambler to get a scent for blood—he was just the first. Soon to follow was "Sleepy Bill" Burns, a former pitcher with a less-than-mediocre 29–55 career record, who got involved with his old friend Cicotte. Burns then involved Billy Maharg, a former fighter from Philadelphia who was a friend and business associate of Burns.

The gamblers needed help financing the operation, which led them to Arnold Rothstein and one of his gofers, former fighter Abe "The Little Champ" Attell. The booty soon increased to $100,000 for the players, as the fixers crossed and double-crossed each other in the process.

As the gamblers raised cash, Gandil continued to recruit coconspirators. One of the last holdouts was Cicotte, who finally agreed to do his part in the fix if he got $10,000 in advance—the amount Comiskey had promised him for winning thirty games.

As game 1 approached, gamblers were betting heavily on the series, in which Chicago was favored 5-to-1 over the Reds. Betting the dog in this series could result in big winnings for gamblers in the know or fans with a hunch.

The White Sox lost the first two games of the series, 9–1 and 4–2. Rumors of a fix became even more rampant, and Ray Schalk and manager Kid Gleason got into heated disputes with Gandil and Williams about their poor play. At this point, the players were to have received $40,000 from Attell, but had received just $10,000. Chicago won game 3, costing gamblers big money. But with Cicotte—who had received the $10,000 he demanded—on the mound for the Sox, the Reds won games 4 and 5.

Down four games to one, after yet another payment was missed, the Sox came back to win games 6 and 7, 5–4 and 4–1. But just one win short of upsetting Chicago, the Reds got an extra boost in what turned out to be the deciding game 8 when Rothstein sent one of his tough guys to make Lefty Williams an offer he couldn't refuse: If he threw the game, he and his wife would not be killed.

Asinof gives a chilling description of Williams's meeting with Rothstein's henchman, known as Harry F. in *Eight Men Out*: "This [Chicago] had been his [Williams] home for four exciting years. He had pitched for this ball club in 144 games. He was twenty-six years old and he thought of himself as a decent man, very good at his job, well liked by those who knew him and worked with him. But Lefty Williams was in trouble. In all his life, he never dreamed that anything like this could happen to him. It seemed so fantastic that even the fact that it was all very logical meant little to him. It would, however, be indelibly recorded in his brain for all time.

"Around 7:30 last evening, Williams and his wife were returning from dinner. He had eaten carefully, knowing he was going to pitch the next day. He had seen him then—a man in a bowler hat, standing at the entrance to his building, smoking a cigar. The man recognized him and immediately got ready to greet him. The man was stiff but polite. He wanted to have a word with him, in private, and a nod indicated to Lefty's wife that she should excuse herself.

"The man went right to the point. He bluntly told Williams he was to lose the next game. Lefty had shaken his head violently and started to turn away. But the man stopped him, restraining him with a vice-like grip on his arm. No, it wasn't a question of money any more. Williams was not going to get paid another dime! He was going to lose that ball game or something was going to happen to him. Maybe something might happen to his wife, too.

"Williams had choked up at the thought of it. His fists had clenched with a sudden desire to tear into the man. But fear had stopped him. He merely stood there, unable to speak or act.

"There was more to the threat. It all had to be done in the first inning. The man eyed him, seeking confirmation of this in Williams's eyes. That's right, the man repeated: Williams was not to last even one inning."

After getting the first out of the inning, Williams surrendered a bloop single to Jack Daubert. With a two-strike count, Heinie Groh singled to right. Williams continued throwing nothing but fastballs, this time to Big Edd Roush, who smashed a double to right field, scoring Daubert. The next hitter, Pat Duncan, batted in two runs with a single to left field, and the Reds were up 3–0. After Williams threw yet another fastball to the next hitter, Larry Kopf, for ball one, Kid Gleason had seen enough and went to the bullpen for reliever Bill James.

Lefty Williams had thrown fifteen pitches and given up four hits and three runs, getting just one out in what was the biggest game of the year. Reliever James gave up a hit, and Cincinnati was up 4–0 in the top half of the first inning.

It was a lead that the White Sox couldn't overcome, and the Reds went on to become World Series champions, beating the heavily favored ChiSox in the Fall Classic. Why the Sox were so heavily favored is a question that remains unanswered, since the Reds had a better regular-season record and won the pennant by a much more comfortable margin than Chicago did.

The stench surrounding the series continued through the following season, until a Chicago grand jury convened in September 1920 to investigate the previous years' Fall Classic. In an September 27 article in the *Philadelphia North American*, Maharg described in detail how Cicotte told him and Burns that Cicotte would throw the series for $100,000. He detailed the double- and triple-crosses that ensued. Cicotte then testified and incriminated his teammates. The Sox, according to Cicotte, also blew the 1920 pennant race, which Cleveland eventually won.

The following June, all eight Sox players were acquitted in their conspiracy trial. But their victory was shallow and short-lived; the very next day, Landis suspended them for life.

The ammunition Joe Jackson's supporters have always used to support his reinstatement and eligibility for the Hall of Fame is that he supposedly wrote a letter to Comiskey after the World Series questioning the play of his teammates and offering to provide details. But the owner of the club never accepted Jackson's offer. Even though he was, at the very least, aware of the fix, his attempts to talk to Comiskey are enough, in many people's eyes, to exonerate him. But it was not enough in the eyes of Kenesaw Mountain Landis—or any subsequent commissioner, as Shoeless Joe remains banished.

Jackson's big-league counterparts respected his ability on the playing field and also formed opinions of his level of involvement, based on their own experiences playing against him and from knowledge they gleaned from other players. In Franz Douskey's article "Smokey

Joe Wood's Last Interview," which appeared in James Charlton's *The National Pastime: A Review of Baseball History*, Wood made some interesting comments about Shoeless Joe.

"He had the reputation and all," Wood said, "and this is only hearsay, that he could not read or write. I know this. Another thing that was told to me that Joe and his roommate would go out for meals. Whatever his roommate ordered, Joe would say, 'Bring me the same,' because he couldn't read the menu. But I don't think Joe Jackson would honestly throw anything. No, no. The ringleader was Chick Gandil. Abe Attell, the prizefighter, was the middleman, so they say. Joe Jackson hit .375 in that series, and he hit the only home run. And he didn't make any errors, so I don't know. You know, we ballplayers used to talk together, and I remember those who played with him considered him the greatest natural hitter there ever was."

Unlike the sympathetic figure that appeared in the movie *Field of Dreams*, Joe Jackson did not pine for baseball after his suspension. He never thought of the game as an appendage that had been amputated,

Joe Jackson showing off some leather. © 2008 Chicago White Sox.

that still itched during the night. In an October 1949 *Sport* magazine article, as told to Furman Bisher, sportswriter for the *Atlanta Journal Constitution*, Shoeless Joe said, "I doubt if I would have gone back into baseball anyway, even if Judge Landis had reinstated me after the trial. I had a good valet business in Savannah Georgia with 22 people working for me and I had to look after it.

"I thought when my trial was over that Judge Landis might have restored me to good standing. But he never did. And until he died I had never gone before him, sent a representative before him, or placed before him any written matter pleading my case. I gave baseball my best and if the game didn't care enough to see me get a square deal, then I wouldn't go out of my way to get back in.

"Baseball failed to keep good faith with me. When I got notice of my suspension three days before the end of the 1920 season—it came on a rained-out day—it read that if found innocent of any wrongdoing, I would be reinstated. If found guilty, I would be banned for life. I was found innocent, and I was still banned for life.

"I was told that Judge Landis had said I was banned because of the company I kept. I roomed with Claude Williams, the pitcher, one of the ringleaders, they told me and one of the eight White Sox players banned. But I had to take whoever they assigned to room with me on the road. I had no power over that.

"Sure I'd heard talk that there was something going on. When the talk got so bad just before the World Series with Cincinnati, I went to Mr. Charles Comiskey's room the night before the World Series started and asked him to keep me out of the line up. Mr. Comiskey was the owner of the White Sox. He refused and I begged him.

"I went out and played my heart out against Cincinnati. I set a record that still stands for the most hits in a Series, though it has been tied, I think. I made 13 hits, but after all the trouble came out they took one away from me. Maurice Rath went over in the hole and knocked down a hot grounder, but he couldn't make a throw on it. They scored it a hit then, but changed it later.

"I led both teams in hitting with .375. I hit the only home run of the Series, off Hod Eller in the last game. I came all the way home from first on a single and scored the winning run in that 5–4 game. I handled 30 balls in the outfield and never made an error or allowed a man to take an extra base. I threw out five men at home and could have had three others, if bad cutoffs hadn't been made. One of them was in the second game Eddie Cicotte lost, when he made two errors in one inning.

"I have read now and then that I am one of the most tragic figures in baseball. Well, Maybe that's the way that some people look at it, but I don't quite see it that way myself. I was 32 years old at the time and I had been in the majors for 13 years. I had a lifetime batting average of .356. I held the all-time throwing record for distance and I had made pretty good salaries for those days. There wasn't much left for me in the big leagues."

The fascinating article also gave Jackson the chance to comment on a myth that came about during the trial. It dealt with the famous "Say it ain't so, Joe" quote.

"I guess the biggest joke of all was that story that got out about 'Say it ain't so, Joe,'" he recounted. "Charley Owens of the *Chicago Daily News* was responsible for that, but there wasn't a bit of truth in it. It was supposed to have happened the day I was arrested in September of 1920, when I came out of the courtroom.

"There weren't any word passed between anybody except me and a deputy sheriff. When I came out of the building, this deputy asked me where I was going and I told him to the Southside. He asked me for a ride and we got in the car together and left. There was a big crowd handing around the front of the building, but nobody else said anything to me. It just didn't happen, that's all. Charley Owens just made up a good story and wrote it. Oh, I would have said it ain't so, all right, just like I'm saying now."

Another player who probably knew about the fix but did not participate was Buck Weaver, who maintained his innocence until his death in 1956. The outstanding third sacker hit .344 in the 1919 World Series, including a triple and four doubles. He also fielded flawlessly. After Weaver's death, a reporter with the Associated Press interviewed the great Ty Cobb about him. Cobb said, "Weaver was the greatest third baseman I ever saw. Buck just wasn't the type to be in a crooked deal like that and certainly there wasn't anything wrong with the way he played in the 1919 World Series."

Landis made it clear that anyone who has knowledge of a fix and does not step forward with the information is as guilty as those involved, and that neither will play professional baseball again. In an interview with James T. Farrell in *My Baseball Diary*, conducted just two years before his death, Weaver spoke about his life.

Buck Weaver in happier times. © 2008 Chicago White Sox.

"Landis wanted me to tell him something that I didn't know," he said. "I can't accuse you and it comes back on you and I am a goof. That makes sense to me. I didn't have any evidence.

"All I can say is the only thing we got left in the world is our judges and our jurors. I was acquitted in court.

"Landis was a funny man. I'd come in. He'd say, 'Sit down, sit down!' He had that big box on his desk full of tobacco. He knew I chewed tobacco, too. He'd give me a chew of tobacco. I appealed I don't know how many times, maybe a half a dozen times. But he never did tell me to my face. I never threw a ball game in my life. All I knew was win. That's all I know.

"A murderer even serves his sentence and is let out. I got life."

Little in life is pure black and white, as many gray areas are usually the norm. While the involvement of Gandil, Cicotte, and Williams is hard to refute, even long after their deaths the involvement of Shoeless Joe Jackson and Buck Weaver is still very much up for debate. It seems evident that, at the very least, they knew of the fix and should have found a way to tell baseball authorities—even though Jackson did try to see Comiskey. That was all that Commissioner Landis needed to hear: that they knew of the fix.

But considering some of the new millennium of scandals that continue to rock baseball up to the present day, it seems unfortunate that two players such as Jackson and Weaver, who got caught up in a bad situation, have not been forgiven and reinstated by baseball. They belong in the Hall of Fame.

In a trial held in 1924 in which Happy Felsch, Swede Risberg, and Joe Jackson sued for back pay, their attorney, Ray Cannon, intended to use information about another, less well-known scandal from just two seasons before the World Series fix. In 1917 the Detroit Tigers lost back-to-back doubleheaders to the White Sox around Labor Day. They also beat Chicago's top rival, the Boston Red Sox, later that season. After the White Sox clinched the pennant, they lost three games to Detroit. The players also had taken up a collection and paid off the Detroit pitchers.

Was the cash a bribe for losing the doubleheaders to the ChiSox? Or was it a reward for beating Boston? And afterward, did Chicago purposely lose the three games to Detroit to help them get closer to third-place money? Landis looked into the situation, but there was apparently never enough evidence to know for sure exactly what had happened.

The 1919 World Series was not the last gambling scandal that rocked the sport. The New York Giants' Jimmy O'Connell supposedly offered Heinie Sand of the Philadelphia Phillies $500 to fix a game in 1924. Landis banned O'Connell and Giants coach Cozy Dolan for life.

In 1926 player-manager Ty Cobb of Detroit and Tris Speaker of Cleveland both resigned their positions due to suspicions that were raised by disgruntled Tiger's pitcher Dutch Leonard, who wrote a letter charging that the two managers were betting on games and fixed a game on September 25, 1919, that enabled Detroit to earn third-place money. Landis held hearings on the matter, but when no evidence was brought forward and Leonard refused to testify, both Cobb and Speaker were reinstated. Then, in 1927, Swede Risberg charged that fifty players knew of the four-game series the Tigers threw to the White Sox in 1917.

Landis banned Phillies owner William D. Cox from the game for betting on Philadelphia games in 1943. And in 1947 Commissioner Albert "Happy" Chandler suspended Brooklyn Dodgers manager Leo "The Lip" Durocher for a year by for conduct detrimental to baseball.

Willie Mays and Mickey Mantle were forced to give up their baseball jobs by Commissioner Bowie Kuhn in order to keep their jobs as casino greeters in Atlantic City. And Detroit pitcher Denny McLain was involved in bookmaking activities in 1970, the first of numerous run-ins baseball's last thirty-game winner had with the law.

Gambling scandals have not been limited to Major League Baseball. In fact, the Black Sox were not the only team accused of fixing baseball games in 1919. The Pacific Coast League's Salt Lake City Bees players Harl Maggert, William Rumler, and Gene Dale were expelled in 1920 for their part in a fix. And Hooper Triplett, an outfielder with the Columbus Cardinals of the Sally League was banned for betting $20 against his team in 1946.

That same season, five players were banned after being accused of throwing playoff games in the Class D Evangeline League. They were Houma Indians manager-first baseman Paul Fugit, third baseman Alvin Kaiser, outfielder Leonard Pecou, and pitcher Bill Thomas; and Abbeville Athletics catcher Don Vettorel.

In 1947 Al McElreath, center fielder for the Muskogee Cardinals of the Class A Western Association, was suspended permanently for attempting to include his teammates in a fix. Even though he insisted the chargers were not true, he cast further doubt on himself by misplaying a ball in the outfield and missing a hit-and-run sign at that plate that led to a base runner being thrown out.

In 1948 pitcher-manager Barney DeForge of Reidsville Luckies in the Class C Carolina League and Emanuel Weingarten, the owner of two teams in other cities, were banned after the pitcher admitted to fixing a game in return for $300. He put himself into a contest that his Reidsville team was trailing by the score of 2–0, then surrendered four walks and hurled a wild pitch, upping the score to 5–0. That score helped beat a run spread that gamblers bet on.

Then, in 1959, in the Southern League, Chattanooga Lookouts first baseman Jess Levan was expelled from baseball for approaching teammates about throwing games. One of the practices that came out of the Levan investigation is that gamblers began to regularly bet on foul balls and involved players who deliberately fouled off pitches. Bookies set odds on whether or not a player would hit a foul on one of the next three pitches.

So while the Black Sox scandal of 1919 was certainly the most famous—or infamous—example of players fixing baseball games, there was a litany of other examples before and after Charles Comiskey's team did the unthinkable.

But the banishing of Pete Rose is a legacy of the fallout over the 1919 scandal. Betting on the game came to be considered a mortal sin in baseball, leading to his being excluded from any chance to be elected to the Hall of Fame, even though his playing career certainly merits that distinction.

Many fans and nonfans alike have difficulty comprehending how ballplayers can now make tens and, in some cases, hundreds of millions of dollars to play baseball. But the dramatic increase in player salaries over the last few decades makes it literally impossible for some of the seedier members of society to bribe a player to throw a game.

3

GAMBLERS NOT SO ANONYMOUS IN BASKETBALL

The Point-Shaving Scandals of 1951

"It was very personal. We all knew these players. It was a very emotional jolt to your psyche. The last thing you expected was that any of these games would be dishonest. This was our connection with what was right, our connection with heroism. Suddenly, we were connected to cheats and guys who sold out the school for a thousand or fifteen hundred dollars. It was very upsetting and embarrassing and emotionally embarrassing."

—Maury Allen

Perhaps more than any other sport, basketball is a target-rich environment for shaving points because of the ease with which a single player or official can influence the outcome of a game—and, even more important, the point spread.

Spread betting, invented in the 1940s by Charles K. McNeil, a mathematics teacher from Connecticut who later became a bookmaker in Chicago, is based on the accuracy of the wager, not just the winner and loser of the particular contest. The point spread is the number of points by which the favored team must win the game, and the bet is whether the outcome will be above or below the spread. So in spread betting, you bet on the difference in score rather than the outcome. For instance, if a good team is playing a much weaker team, most of those betting on the game would favor the stronger team to the extent that very few bets would be placed on the weak team. The point spread, in effect, gives a "handicap" to the weaker team, which entices more action by making it attractive to place bets on either team.

As an example, suppose a game has a spread of 5 points. If the gambler bets the favorite, he is giving the points. So not only must his team win, but it must win by more than 5 points. If the gambler bets the underdog, he is taking the points and will win if the underdog wins the game or loses by fewer than 5 points. If the difference in the two teams' scores matches the point spread, that is known as a push and no money is won or lost.

One of the dangers of sports betting is that it can easily lead to attempts to shave points. Point shaving usually involves sports gamblers and one or more players of the team favored to win the game. In exchange for a bribe, the player or players agree to ensure that their team will not win by the margin required by the spread, or "cover the spread." The gambler then bets against the favored team, which can still win the game, but not by the points needed to cover the spread. Players from a favored team can also try to influence the spread by running up the score to beat a weaker team by a larger margin than the spread.

The revelation in 2007 that NBA referee Tim Donaghy made calls intended to affect the point spread of games he had bet on is just the latest black mark on basketball caused by the irrefutable influence of gambling on the sport. While most NBA players are thought to be safe from the temptations to dishonestly affect the outcomes of games and point spreads because of their astronomical salaries, the same could never be said for college athletes. Probably the most known scandal in all of sport is the 1919 White Sox purposely throwing the World Series. But a close second has to be the City College of New York (CCNY) point-shaving scandal that came to light in 1951. The scandal ran so deep that it nearly destroyed college basketball.

In what seemed like one of the great Herculean stories in the history of college athletics, the unranked CCNY squad of 1949–50 earned a berth in the National Invitational Tournament (NIT) by the skin of their collective teeth following the Beavers' 17–5 regular season. The Beavers opened the NIT by defeating defending champion San Francisco before meeting Adolph Rupp and his third-ranked

Kentucky Wildcats, winners of the 1948 and 1949 NCAA tournaments and considered one of the greatest college teams ever.

Fans of the Beavers had a unique chant they used to show their support of the team. They shouted, "allagaroo-garoo-garah, allagaroo-garoo-garah, ee-yah, sis-boom-bah!" The chant was thought to be a cross between an alligator and a kangaroo, or a takeoff on the French phrase *allez guerre*, meaning "on to the war."

Led by their starting five of Floyd Lane, Al "Fats" Roth, Ed Roman, Ed Warner, and Irwin Dambrot, coach Nat Holman's squad opened a 45–20 lead over Rupp's Kentucky team at halftime. They never looked back. Next the Beavers defeated sixth-ranked Duquesne and then top-ranked Bradley in the championship game at Madison Square Garden in New York in front of eighteen thousand fans. Ten days later, CCNY once again defeated Bradley at the Garden to win the NCAA tournament. History and adulation was theirs, as no team had ever won both the NIT and NCAA championships during the same season.

But that history and adulation turned to shame and pain in 1951, when seven CCNY players and twenty-three more from six other schools were arrested and charged with accepting money to fix games between 1947 and 1950. The investigation concluded that three of the five games that CCNY lost during the regular season in 1950 were fixed and that points were shaved in others. All seven CCNY players—Roth (sentenced to six months in a workhouse, but the sentence was suspended when he entered the U.S. Army), Warner (sentenced to six months in jail), Roman (suspended sentence), Herb Cohen (suspended sentence), Dambrot (suspended sentence), Norman Mager (suspended sentence), and Lane (suspended sentence)—were found guilty.

The scandal rocked the campus of CCNY, which was originally founded in 1847 by Townsend Harris as a combination prep school and college. A well-respected academic institution, it was also a melting pot that accepted students from all races and religions. In the years when many top private schools admitted only children of the Protestant establishment, many brilliant students of other religions—especially Jewish students—attended City College, which was, in many cases, their only option.

"The school was special," says broadcaster Marvin Kalb, class of 1951. "The student body was special. The environment was special.

The sense of having to achieve was special and the people on the team were also special, because there were Jewish kids on the team and there were black kids on the team. The idea of a WASP being on the team was literally unheard of. So you were dealing with minorities who had to make it. So there was that kind of psychological as well as physical energy behind everything the team did."

No other public college has produced as many Nobel laureates; nine are alumni of the college. The educational excellence of what is looked at as a working-class school has resulted in nicknames such as "Harvard of the Proletariat," "the poor man's Harvard," and "Harvard on Hudson."

Just some of the notable graduates of City College include former New York City mayor Ed Koch; former U.S. Senator Robert F. Wagner Sr.; film director Stanley Kubrick; actors Judd Hirsch, Edward G. Robinson, and Ray Romano; authors Mario Puzo and Bernard Malamud; and famed basketball coach Red Holzman. Another graduate is author Maury Allen, of the class of 1953.

"We used to call City College the Harvard of the poor," Allen says of his alma mater. "It was a free tuition school—a very difficult school to get into. You had to have a combined average of over 85 in high school and over an 85 in an exam they gave you. It was difficult to get in, but you had exceptional students. It was very academic. Everybody seemed to be politically active in those post–World War II days. It was kind of a question of where the country was going.

"The school had a lot of activism and some very liberal attitudes present there. A lot of demonstrations were held against teachers who certain students thought were racists. There were a couple of school strikes, but it was a historic college that started in the 1840s. It was a very distinguished place and a lot of well-known, famous people attended and graduated. It was quite prestigious to attend there."

While the Beavers were not the only team hit by the scandal, the effect of the revelations on CCNY and its fans was devastating. There was a bond that united this collection of students of all races and creeds, including Jews, blacks, and Catholics. They were the children of immigrants and slaves. Just the thought that their fellow students could sell out their honor in such a way hit home in a particularly hard way. When the truth came out—that the players had taken money to help gamblers win big money—a trust was lost. The team and its fans were forced to grow up early as a result of the scandal.

"It was very depressing, very upsetting," says Allen. "Two things gave you status as a City College student. First, you considered yourself an exceptional student, and second, the basketball team was the instrument that gave the school national attention. In New York everyone knew about City College. But there wasn't any TV in those days, and people didn't know about the eastern schools outside of the New York area. The basketball team gave the school a great deal of status and recognition. Any undergraduate like myself felt a part of that. You went to a great school, and a great basketball school too. The kids from Harvard and Yale couldn't say that.

"It was very personal. We all knew these players. It was a very emotional jolt to your psyche. The last thing you expected was that any of these games would be dishonest. This was our connection with what was right, our connection with heroism. Suddenly, we were connected to cheats and guys who sold out the school for a thousand or fifteen hundred dollars. It was very upsetting and embarrassing and emotionally embarrassing."

The incidents of point shaving came to light on January 17, 1951, when two members of the Manhattan College team, Henry Poppe and Jack Byrnes, were booked on bribery and conspiracy charges. They were booked along with Cornelious Kelleher and brothers Benjamin and Irving Schwartzberg, who were convicted felons and bookmakers. They were in violation of section 382 of the penal code, which established as illegal an attempt to bribe a participant in any sporting event, amateur or professional. The incident on January 17 was a harbinger of things to come in the year that nearly ruined college basketball. It seemed as if every month had new allegations, arrests, and disillusionment.

On February 18, CCNY players Warner, Roman, and Roth were arrested in New York City's Penn Station after the team returned from Philadelphia, where the Beavers had beaten Temple, 95–71. The three were charged with bribery.

Two days after that bombshell, Long Island University players Sherman White, LeRoy Smith, and Adolph Bigos were arrested for taking bribes from fixer Salvatore "Tarto" Sollazzo, via former LIU player Eddie Gard, to throw games. Ironically, the day before his arrest, White had been named the *Sporting News* Player of the Year.

The following month, on March 26, the final CCNY players involved in the scam, Irwin Dambrot and Norm Cohen, were arrested.

Then, in April, fixer Eli Klukofsky was arrested for bribing CCNY players in the 1949–50 season; he was arrested again in July for bribing Toledo University players Bill Waller, Carlo Muzi, Bob McDonald, and Jack Freeman. Klukofsky died of a heart attack during his trial. Another LIU player, Jackie Goldsmith, was arrested on July 22, 1951, for his role in fixing games with Gard.

New revelations of the scandal continued to mount in July, when Gene Melchiorre, Bill Mann, Bud Grover, Aaron Preece, and Jim Kelly of Bradley University all admitted to accepting bribes from gamblers to hold down scores against St. Joseph's in Philadelphia and Oregon State, in Chicago. The following month, gamblers Nick and Tony Englises, Joe Benintende, and Jack West were indicted.

The point-shaving scandal wound cut deep into the basketball heart of the nation. One of the sport's most successful coaches was Adolph Rupp of Kentucky. He bragged that his team would never be party to such a temptation. Yet his squad was tarnished as well. His claims that "they couldn't reach my boys with a ten-foot-pole" were all wrong. In fact, his "boys" were every bit as guilty as the teams from New York.

"The scandal dramatically affected Rupp's career and effectively placed a barrier on his accomplishments," says University of Kentucky researcher and writer Jon Scott. "His decision to stay on at UK, rather than retire, which was what many assumed he would do due to poor health, was in keeping with his personal beliefs of working through adversity and to answer critics through victory.

"But it came at a great cost. He no longer was the darling of the media and, although well known, was no longer widely popular outside the state of Kentucky. Although he went on to become the winningest coach of all time and is still arguably one of the greatest basketball coaches ever, his legacy lost much of its luster."

As 1951 wound down, the onslaught continued when Ralph Beard, Alex Groza, and Dale Barnstable of Kentucky were arrested for accepting $500 each to shave points in an NIT game against Loyola of Chicago in Madison Square Garden in 1949. Previously that year they also played to affect the point spread in games against De Paul, Vanderbilt, and Tennessee. Former UK football player Nick Englises and his associates approached Beard, Groza, and Barnstable in late 1948 about beating a point spread, which they did, for $100, against St. John's. The Wildcats were involved from that point forward.

"Those guys [Englises and his cohorts] were smooth talkers," Barnstable said in Charlie Rosen's *Scandals of '51*. "They should have been salesmen. They took us out for a stroll, treated us to a meal, and before we knew anything, we were right in the middle of it. They said we didn't have to dump the game. They said nobody would get hurt except other gamblers. They said everybody was doing it. And they asked what was wrong with winning a game by as many points as we could. We just didn't think. But if somebody suspected what was going on at the Garden had warned us that things like that were against the law, we'd never have done it."

In a 1952 article in *True* magazine, Englises said it was Groza who was most interested in cashing in on his basketball skills. But both Groza and Beard vehemently objected to this version of what occurred.

Another member of the team, All-American center Bill Spivey, was barred from athletic play at the university on March 2, 1952. From the beginning, he always maintained his innocence. "I could not have been involved in such fixing because of my loyalty to my school, to the people who believed in me and because of my love for the game," he said in *Scandals of '51*.

Two of Spivey's former teammates, Jim Line and Walter Hirsch, testified under oath that he was a willing participant in the point shaving. But Spivey repeatedly claimed, also while under oath, that he was innocent of fixing games. He did state that he was approached two times, but had refused. His greatest sin, much like that of baseball's Shoeless Joe Jackson, was that he did not report the offer. Spivey even passed a lie detector test in which he claimed he was not involved in the fixing.

The university refused to reinstate Spivey because officials believed he was involved in fixing a game that UK lost to St. Louis, 43–42. But in that game the seven-footer led all scorers, with 16 points, and made eight of ten free throws.

Spivey was not convicted of any wrongdoing; his perjury trial ended in a mistrial, as the jury favored his acquittal by a 9–3 margin. Years later, he returned to the university to complete his college degree. It was important to Spivey that he be handed his diploma by UK president Herman Donovan—the man who had suspended him from the team.

Although Spivey was never convicted, the NBA would not allow Spivey to play. He sued the NBA for $800,000, settling out of court for $10,000.

"The aftershocks of the scandal severely damaged not only the Kentucky program, but its players as well," says Jon Scott. "Not only were the accomplishments of UK's and the nation's most beloved team, The Fabulous Five, tarnished, but the lives of the players were altered dramatically, just when they were starting to realize their dreams in the NBA. Many of these players likely would have become Hall-of-Fame multimillionaire owners of an NBA franchise, but saw it evaporate before their eyes.

"The fact the seven-foot All-American Bill Spivey sat out the 1951–52 season waiting for word on his case prevented a likely national championship opportunity and also the chance to compete for the 1952 Olympic team, a similar feat to what Kentucky accomplished in 1948. The suspension also prevented another likely national championship run with Cliff Hagan and Frank Ramsey, who were graduate students and therefore unable to play in the postseason. So to say that Kentucky paid for its transgressions is an understatement.

"Long term, the 1951 scandal and Kentucky's decision to stick with their coach, Adolph Rupp, in many ways helped define the program going forward. By choosing to remain competitive at the highest levels of college basketball, they opened themselves to criticism and became an open target for the NCAA.

"This is the reality that they have to deal with even today. No matter how clean they run their program today or for how long, as long as UK remains successful and competitive in college basketball, their critics will be sure to hold past misdeeds against them."

A list of college players arrested as a result of the investigation almost reads like a roster of possible All-Americans: Al Roth, Ed Warner, Ed Roman, Herb Cohen, Irwin Dambrot, Norman Mager, and Floyd Lane of CCNY; Natie Miller, Lou Lipman, Adolph Bigos, Dick Feurtado, LeRoy Smith, and Sherman White of LIU; Gene Melchiorre, Bill Mann, George Chianakos, Bud Grover, Aaron Preece, Jim Kelly, and Fred Schlictman of Bradley; Connie Schaaf of New York University; Dale Barnstable, Ralph Beard, and Alex Groza of Kentucky; Jack Byrnes and Henry Poppe of Manhattan; Bill Waller,

Carlo Muzi, Bob McDonald, and Jack Freeman of Toledo; and Eddie Gard and Jackie Goldsmith of LIU. Most of the players were given suspended sentences. Grover, Preece, Kelly, and Schlictman were all acquitted, and charges were dropped against Toledo players Waller, Muzi, McDonald, and Freeman.

The wheels of justice were not as kind to the fixers and gamblers. Salvatore Sollazzo was sentenced to eight to sixteen years in state prison. Irving Schwartzberg, Benjamin Schwartzberg, and Cornelius Kelleher were all sentenced to one year in prison. Jack West received two to three years, Joe Benitende got four to seven years, and Nick Englises received up to three years. Tony Englises was sentenced to six months, while Eli Klukofsky suffered a fatal heart attack while awaiting trial.

While many of the players involved in the scandal have kept to themselves in the years since and have not spoken publicly about their roles, CCNY's Norm Mager discussed what happened in a 1996 interview with Ira Berkow of the *New York Times*. He painted a portrait of a young man who clearly didn't understand the repercussions of his actions; he had no idea just how his involvement would affect the rest of his life.

"For a long time I didn't talk about the scandals," said Mager, who passed away in 2005. "For what? I went into my father's building maintenance business and I was useless. I'd sit there downcast. When people asked if I was Norm Mager, I'd say no. I didn't tell my kids about it, and that caused a problem. When my second wife got a call from a newspaper saying they were going to run a story about the scandals, she threatened to sue them when I got home. I had never told her. And I said, 'No, honey, it's true.'

"Eventually, I started to get over it. We were just dumb, naïve, kids, 19, 20 years old. We didn't know of any law that said you shouldn't shave points—we weren't throwing games, after all. And we thought, hell, the money looked pretty good. Even if it wasn't a lot, it seemed like a lot to us, since we had almost nothing.

"I look at the money kids in college are getting today, and what we got was like peanuts. I'm not condoning what we did—it was wrong—but times change."

Sadly, the 1951 scandals are not the only black mark on college basketball. In 1961 St. Joseph's University had to relinquish its third-place finish in the NCAA tournament when a student athlete was alleged to have been involved with a gambler. The following year, in 1962, another major scandal implicated thirty-seven players from twenty-two institutions, resulting in the arrest and conviction of three gamblers who were charged with fixing college basketball games.

Tulane University ended its basketball program after five players were accused of point shaving in a pair of games in 1985. Among those arrested was John "Hot Rod" Williams, who was accused of pocketing more than $8,000 for shaving points. Williams was indicted on five criminal counts, but, after a mistrial, charges were dropped. The school reinstated its basketball team in the 1989–90 season.

In 1992, nineteen football and basketball student athletes from the University of Maine were suspended for participating in a gambling operation.

In 1994 a comprehensive point-shaving scheme involving former Arizona State basketball players Steven Smith and Isaac Burton Jr. was discovered. The pair pleaded guilty to charges of conspiracy to commit sports bribery.

Finally, in 1998, a student approached a men's basketball student athlete at California State University at Fullerton and offered him $1,000 to shave points in an upcoming game. The player cooperated with authorities and the student was arrested on felony point-shaving charges after the player assisted police in a sting operation. Happily, sometimes the players do the right thing.

One final note about the players from CCNY who were involved in the scandal that rocked college basketball nearly sixty years ago:

"There was a lot of talk after the scandal that some of the players involved got in the school because they were basketball players and there was some indications that records might have been tampered with," says Maury Allen. "But most of them went on to very successful professional careers. Ed Roman was a school principal. Floyd Lane was a teacher. Irwin Dambrot was a successful dentist. Al Roth made a lot of money in business. They were a successful group of students. They got into the school because they were top students."

Every Beaver player involved in the scandal went back to school and earned his degree. They all deserve one final chant for that accomplishment.

"Allagaroo-garoo-garah, allagaroo-garoo-garah, ee-yah, sis-boombah."

4

BASEBALL

Spit, Corks, Periscopes, & Superstitions

"If you believe you're playing well because you're getting
laid, or because you're not getting laid, or because you're
wearing women's underwear, then you are. And you should
know that."

—Crash Davis to Annie Savoy in *Bull Durham*

There are many reasons baseball has become America's Game. There
is the leisurely pace, which often camouflages the layers of sophisticated strategy that is present before each and every pitch. The atmosphere at a ballpark makes it possible for adults to escape the
stresses of the real world and once again feel like children. And then
there is the long and proud history of baseball, which offers a wide-
ranging social commentary that often reflects the world outside the
white lines. But at the end of the day, it is what occurs between the
white lines that is still the draw that makes America's Pastime the best
game on the planet.

It seems that there is always someone trying to get the upper hand
in life by taking the easy, dishonest route. We have already discussed
the greed of gamblers who have made their presence felt in affecting
point spreads and at least one World Series. The sobering realization
that baseball and other sports have finally come to grips with concerning the use of steroids and other performance-enhancing drugs
will be treated in later chapters. But an interesting and entertaining

aspect of the history of baseball deals with some of the innovative and inventive ways that players and teams have played folly with the rules of the game to gain an unfair advantage, without the help of a hypodermic needle.

The history of the game is replete with examples of skirting the rules. Do instances such as these qualify as cheating? Of course they do. But compared to some of the revelations of juiced athletes competing on an unnatural and unfair playing field, these old-fashioned types of cheating almost seem like a welcome throwback to a simpler time when all was right with the world. Whether you call it cheating or gamesmanship, the practice has been present in baseball from the start—always has been and always will be. Make no mistake, in baseball, it is an art form.

There are countless examples of players and managers taking it to the limit—and sometimes over it.

Jerry Casway, writer and historian. Photo courtesy of Jerry Casway.

"In the nineteenth Century, the most successful teams were those who played the Irish or Baltimore style of play," says Jerrold Casway. "A lot of it was originated with Charlie Comiskey, who learned it from Ted Sullivan. Their thing was to try to get a competitive edge. A lot of the strategies about cutting off throws, or playing off the bag were introduced, that were looked at as cheating at first. But they were getting a competitive edge. Ned Hanlon of Baltimore learned it from Comiskey; Hughie Jennings and John McGraw then picked it up.

"In the Murphy brothers book [*Level Playing Fields: How The Groundskeeping Murphy Brothers Shaped Baseball*, by Peter Morris], about tending the baseball diamond, they would wet the dirt in front of home plate so a bunt would go dead. In Baltimore, one of the first teams under Hanlon started playing around with the pitcher's mound. It later became part of the game. One of the things the Orioles did was put soap shavings around the mound. That way, when an opposing pitcher went down for some dirt to dry his sweaty hands, it would be slippery. Then they would have someone in the outfield with mirrors to make it hard to see. McGraw used to grab people's belts when they went around third base. He was just getting that competitive edge, like the social Darwinism of the period. It's the survival of the fittest.

"This was mostly practiced by the Irish. Connie Mack, Charlie Comiskey, Ned Hanlon, and John McGraw were all Irish. One of the things the Orioles perfected was taking advantage of having only one umpire. Sometimes a coach would break for home, which would distract the fielders. Then Mike 'King' Kelly would run from first to third across the field when the umpire's back was turned. All of these things didn't hurt anybody, but they are all to get an edge. Like looking to see which pitch was coming and stealing signs. Is it cheating? It is."

Baseball is a particularly interesting sport, because there are very few examples of what exactly is right and wrong. Where do you draw the line? Umpires are in a unique situation in sports. They often view occurrences that they keep to themselves unless one of the teams brings them to the attention of the umpire.

"If you look at the historical background of baseball, the game itself is played so you get away with anything you can that the umpire can't detect, unlike golf, where you police yourself," says Jim Evans, who enjoyed a twenty-eight-year career as a major-league umpire, nineteen of which he spent as an American League crew chief. After his retirement, he founded the Jim Evans Academy of Professional Umpiring. "There is really only one group of honest athletes in the world, and that's the golfers. Tom Kite once called a penalty on himself that cost him one of the major tournaments. You just don't see that in other sports.

"In most sports, like basketball, football, or baseball, they never think that they are out or committed a penalty. You don't see a base runner say he was really out when an umpire calls him safe. In baseball, you have a doctrine of constant vigilance. It's up to the defensive team to catch an offensive mistake or error. It's the responsibility of the defensive team to make certain appeal plays, such as batting out of order. If the umpire notices it, he doesn't call it to anyone's attention. Another example of that is the failure to retouch properly if you leave a base too early on a sacrifice fly ball. The base runner doesn't have to retouch if the defensive team doesn't appeal it. And if the umpire sees it and nobody else does, he just keeps quiet."

One of the first things that comes to mind when a discussion about cheating in baseball occurs when a pitcher doctors the baseball in some way so that it will react in a different way than batters are expecting. Early in the history of baseball, a pitcher's job was not to fool the hitter or even try to get him out; rather, his job was to throw the ball in a way and to an area where the batter could hit it. In fact, the batter—or

Umpire Jim Evans separates Boston's Manny Ramirez from Jeff Weaver, who plunked him with a pitch. Photo courtesy of Jim Evans.

Umpire Jim Evans
restrains Yankee
Skipper Billy Martin.
Photo courtesy of
Jim Evans.

striker, as they were known as in those days—would indicate where he would like the ball thrown. Eventually, the competitiveness of the pitchers came into play as they began what is now the tradition of trying to fool the batter by throwing pitches that deceive him.

Anything a pitcher can do to change the aerodynamics of the flight of a pitched baseball is fair game—at least in the mind of the pitcher. Thus, they utilize the curveball, slider, slip pitch, changeup, circle change, knuckleball, forkball, palm ball, split-finger fastball, knuckle curve, screwball, and countless other variations of these pitches that can all be thrown at different speeds, adding a whole new repertoire to the pitcher's arsenal. As an earlier generation of hitters had to deal with the increasing ability of a pitcher to actually try to deceive them, the hurlers began to take the art of deception to new levels at the turn of the twentieth century. It was then that they discovered that by adding saliva or some other substance to a baseball, or cut the ball, it would react violently and differently, making good contact by the hitter even more difficult.

What makes the spitball spit? Or, more correctly, what does doctoring a baseball do to make it react in such a manner? Derek Zumsteg explained the phenomenon in *The Cheater's Guide to Baseball*.

"Spitballs have been used in two ways," he wrote. "First and most commonly, the pitcher uses a conventional fastball grip, with his fingertips on the wet spot. As the ball comes off the pitcher's hand, it slips off the fingers. The effect is almost the same as with a knuckle ball, as the ball is thrown with little spin. And like a knuckle ball, it's notorious for diving down toward the plate late in flight.

"The second use of a spitball is entirely different. Using a lubricant that decreases air friction on one side, the pitch will generate the same kind of break a curve does, toward the side the lubricant is on, and can be thrown at full speed. You can see that this would be highly valued for a pitcher and amazingly frustrating for a hitter.

"Cutting or scuffing a ball to create a rough spot has the opposite effect, causing the ball to move away from the direction of the rough spot. Scuff the left side and the ball will go to the right; scuff the right side and it will move to the left."

Larry Dierker, an outstanding major-league pitcher, manager, and announcer who has spent more than forty years in baseball, had a front row seat to observe those who skirted the rules of baseball during his long career with the Houston Astros and the St. Louis Cardinals. He has seen it all, and has an understanding of just how doctoring the baseball can be an effective part of a pitcher's repertoire on the mound.

"There are several ways a pitcher can cheat," Dierker says. "If he throws a spitball, he is using some slick substance on the tips of his throwing fingers. He can get the moisture from his mouth, or from a clear, oily substance that has been applied to the uniform or the skin. When you throw a spitball, the ball squirts out of your grip like a wet bar of soap, with very little spin. So it's kind of like a knuckleball, but doesn't dance as much because it is thrown much harder. It is actually more like a really fast split-finger fastball. The loose spin seems to make it lurch downward as it approaches the hitting area. The advantage of a spitball is that you can throw it almost as hard as your fastball, and it is relatively easy to control. I threw one when I was warming up on the side one day when I was young and could throw pretty hard. The catcher didn't appreciate it because I didn't tell him I was going to do it, and it handcuffed him.

Larry Dierker, player, manager, announcer, and writer. Photo courtesy of Larry Dierker.

"Another way to cheat is by doctoring the ball so that there will be more wind resistance on one side than the other. If you scuff it, it will move away from the scuffed side. A pitcher can attach an abrasive material to his glove or his hand to do the scuffing, and it is hard to see him do it as almost every pitcher rubs the ball to get a better grip. Obviously, most of them are not scuffing the ball. I heard that Whitey Ford and Lew Burdette would get a smudge of dirt from the mound onto the side of the ball and naturally there would be more wind resistance on that side. But I'd have to see that to believe it. I know the ball would move, but I can't imagine how a pitcher could get the dirt on the ball without everyone seeing him do it.

"I never used anything illegal in a game. It's not that I had a moral or ethical objection to it. It was more a case of not needing it. When I went down, I went down fast. In fact, I went from not needing it to not throwing well enough for it to do me any good in a very short span of time.

"Another trick that some pitchers have used is pitching from slightly in front of the rubber. They just rock back, and then step forward maybe six inches in front of the rubber, thus shortening the distance to home plate."

The late Richie Ashburn—a Hall of Fame outfielder, announcer, and writer who played for the Philadelphia Phillies, Chicago Cubs, and New York Mets—once said of pitchers: "After fifteen years of facing them, you don't really get over them. They're devious. They're the only players in the game allowed to cheat. They throw illegal pitches, and they sneak foreign substances on the ball. They can inflict pain whenever they wish. And they're the only ones on the diamond who have high ground. That's symbolic. You know what they tell you in war—'Take the high ground first.'"

Ashburn also was known to tell his daughters that, while in his opinion it was all right to marry a baseball player, he would not have a pitcher for a son-in-law. His daughters knew he was not kidding.

"The whole art of pitching is controlling the spin on the ball," says Evans. "Any time you have an abrasion on the surface, it changes the behavior of the ball. Certain players have a reputation. A lot of it is psychological. They want the reputation of being a cheater even if they are not. A lot of the gimmicks that Gaylord Perry did with his hair, sideburns, and the back of his neck were diversionary tactics. You play psychological warfare with the hitter and create doubt. He might only throw one or two spitballs the entire game, maybe to get a ground ball double play in a crucial situation. But for every hitter up there, that will be his excuse.

"KY Jelly was the grease of choice for a while because it's odorless and invisible. Rub it on your skin and it comes up with the perspiration. As an umpire, you want tangible proof even though you can detect an illegal pitch by the flight of the ball. You want evidence on the baseball. If you find an unnatural cut, you collect two or three balls with evidence of unnatural wear and tear on the ball, and you show the pitcher one of the balls. You'll say to the pitcher, 'I'm not accusing you of anything, but I've got three baseballs with cuts on the same place. If you're doing it, you'd better stop.'

"Back in the 1970s, Perry challenged the league and the umpire supervisor who flew in for one of his games. He put on a demonstration in the bullpen showing his split-finger fastball that acted like a spitter. He could throw a ball that had some real funky breaks. A lot of people mistook it for a spitter. He demonstrated it for them and they agreed that it had the same characteristics as a spitter. He built a good case.

"I made him change his shirt one time in a game in Oakland because it was soaking wet. He thanked me and said he had run out of stuff on the wet shirt. One time I found a guy putting foreign substances on his crucifix. It would pop out from under his jersey with each pitch. During a television commercial I warned him, because you don't usually wear Vasoline on your crucifix."

When it first came into being, the spitball was not illegal. While many pitchers used the spitter to varying degrees, the pitch soon became a popular weapon in a hurler's arsenal. A look at the history of the pitch shows a long ancestry, like most other elements of baseball.

The history of the spitball probably goes as far back as the days when pitchers were forced to throw underhand tosses to the hitters' liking. Wetting their fingers made it possible to grip the ball a little better and to make it a little tougher for the hitter, because the ball would act differently. While it is virtually impossible to trace the thrower of the first spitter, as far back as 1884 the diminutive pitcher Bobby Mathews, who was just five-foot-five and 140 pounds, had three consecutive thirty-win seasons. According to Peter Morris, in his fascinating book *A Game of Inches: The Game on the Field*, two knowledgeable and respected sportswriters credit Mathews as the father of the spitter.

In an article that appeared in the *Sporting News* on November 4, 1909, Tim Murnane wrote, "Bobby Mathews became a famous pitcher by what is now known as the spit ball." He mirrored the sentiments of William Rankin, who wrote in the *Sporting News* on February 13, 1908, "There is no doubt that Mathews was the originator of the spit ball. He used to rub the ball on the breeches until there was a white spot or one much lighter than the rest of the ball, and then wet his finger. He used to say the grass made the ball slippery, that was why he rubbed it on his breeches, and then he wet his fingers to get a good hold on the ball."

Other pitchers known to wet their fingers before pitching included Tommy Bond, Mickey Welch, Charley Buffington, James "Pud" Galvin, and Charley Radbourn. But it wasn't until after the turn of the century that the art of the spitball was taught and shared.

As Morris noted in *A Game of Inches*: "And so the spitball would seem to have resulted from a tag-team effort by several men in the first few years of the twentieth century. Frank Corridon had used it but not appreciated it; George Hildebrand realized what it was and showed it to Elmer Stricklett; Stricklett mastered it and shared it with many others, including Jack Chesbro and Ed Walsh; Chesbro and Walsh brought the pitch to its highest level of attainment.

"Billy Hallman maintained in 1907 that Stricklett may have perfected the pitch, 'but he never discovered it. Long before Stricklett was heard of in base ball, catcher Frank Bowerman had it. When he was with Baltimore in the old National League days he used to use this same ball to have fun with the boys. One day he called me up to play throw and catch and commenced smearing the ball with spit. He called my attention to the way it fooled a fellow and we had considerable fun over it.'"

In *Pitching in a Pinch*, Hall of Fame pitcher Christy Mathewson wrote, "Bowerman, the old Giant catcher, was throwing the spit ball for two or three years before it was discovered to be a pitching asset. He used to wet his fingers when catching, and as he threw to second base the ball would take all sorts of eccentric breaks which fooled the baseman, and no one could explain why it did until Stricklett came through with the spit ball."

Whatever its origins, led by the likes of Chesbro and Walsh, the pitch became a mainstay of the dead ball era, where runs were hard to come by and pitching dominated the sport. But as the second decade of the twentieth century wound down, a number of influences put the use of the spitball in question. There was a growing group of people who were offended by the unsanitary aspects of the pitch. World War I had ended, which meant an influx of reenergized baseball fans coming back from war were giving more attention to the game. Toward the end of the 1920 season, revelations about eight members of the Chicago White Sox conspiring to fix the 1919 World Series came to light. All of these factors, plus the desire to see more offense in the game—along with the maturation of a young star in the making, George Herman "Babe" Ruth—were all converging on the game at the same time. But it was a tragic incident on August 16, 1920, that forever changed the game and led to the illegalization of the spitball.

The Cleveland Indians opposed the New York Yankees that day as Stan Coveleski took the mound for the Tribe, opposed by a hard-throwing spitball specialist with a nasty side-arm motion, Carl Mays of the Yankees. With the Indians trying to avenge a four-game sweep by the Yanks in a recent series in Cleveland, the visitors enjoyed a 3–0 lead going into the top of the fifth inning. Mays prepared to face off against shortstop Ray Chapman.

Mays had a reputation for being a mean pitcher who would quite often dust a batter off with inside pitches. Chapman was a scrappy player who crowded the plate in a crouched stance and was often hit by pitches. As he led off the fifth inning, Chapman was possibly expecting Mays to start him off with a breaking ball away. But Mays threw his first pitch high and inside, literally freezing Chapman, who never moved away from the pitch.

He was hit on the left side of his head, and the sound of the impact of the baseball resonated throughout the Polo Grounds. Of course, in 1920, batting helmets were not used. Blood ran out of his ears, mouth, and nose.

As medical personnel and teammates rushed to his aid, Chapman lay unconscious on the ground. He was, however, revived and tried to walk off the field into the dugout, but began to collapse and was carried off the field by his Indians teammates.

X-rays at the hospital showed that Chapman had suffered a depressed fracture on the left side of his skull. His condition grew steadily worse throughout the evening, and surgery was performed just after midnight, even though Chapman's wife had not yet arrived in New York. Surgeons removed a piece of the player's skull during the hour-long operation.

Although his immediate response to the surgery was encouraging, Ray Chapman died at 4:40 a.m. on August 17, 1920.

As a result of Ray Chapman's tragic death, baseball made some basic changes to the way the game was played. The established practice of often using the same baseball for an entire game ended. Now new balls were used, and dirty or scuffed baseballs were replaced. This made the ball much easier for batters to see, particularly at twilight. Keep in mind that in those days all games were played during the day and there were no lights on fields.

A new rule was also introduced that made it illegal for a pitcher or any other player to doctor the baseball, making pitches such as the spitball, shine ball, and grease ball illegal after the 1920 season.

The rule reads: "In the event of the ball being intentionally discolored by any player, either by rubbing it with the soil, or by applying rosin, paraffin, licorice, or any other foreign substance to it, or otherwise intentionally damaging or roughening the same with sandpaper or emery paper, or other substance, the umpire shall forthwith demand the return of that ball and substitute it for another legal ball, and the offending player shall be disbarred from further participation in the game."

Seventeen pitchers who regularly used the spitball—Burleigh Grimes, Doc Ayers, Ray Caldwell, Stan Coveleski, Bill Doak, Phil Douglas, Red Faber, Dana Fillingim, Ray Fisher, Marv Goodwin, Dutch Leonard, Clarence Mitchell, Jack Quinn, Dick Rudolph, Allen Russell, Urban Shocker, and Allen Sothoron—were granted exemptions that allowed them to keep throwing the pitch until they retired. Grimes would be the last pitcher to earn a major-league victory throwing a legal spitball, with the Pittsburgh Pirates in 1934.

One thing that did not change in the game as a result of Chapman's death was the use of batting helmets. Eleven seasons passed before Pee Wee Reese and Joe Medwick of the Brooklyn Dodgers first wore batting helmets, on March 7, 1941.

So with the exception of those seventeen hurlers, it was now illegal for a pitcher to throw a spitball. This was particularly unfortunate for Pittsburgh Pirates right-hander Hal Carlson. Although he was an avid user of the spitball, for some reason the Pirates failed to register him with the league as a spitball artist who could continue to use the pitch. As a result, he had to reinvent his repertoire on the mound.

One of the greatest spitball pitchers of all time, Preacher Roe of the Brooklyn Dodgers, not only could throw the pitch, but could control it and never get caught.

After baseball changed its rules about doctoring balls, ensuing generations of players had to circumvent the rules if they wanted to throw the pitch. And whether they admit guilt or not, many hurlers have been caught wet-handed throwing spitballs and defacing balls in other ways. The first pitcher to get the gate for ten games—on July 20, 1944—was Nels Potter of the St. Louis Browns. In the midst of a pennant-winning season in which Potter sported a 19–7 record, he was ejected from the game and suspended when he ignored umpire Cal Hubbard's orders not to wet his fingers before going to the resin bag. Potter denied his guilt.

The second pitcher on the list was Phillies reliever John Boozer, who was ejected from a game on May 2, 1968, by umpire Ed

Vargo for throwing spitballs during his warm-up pitches. That's right—his warm-up pitches. After the first time Boozer went to his mouth, the umpire called a ball, even though no batter was in the box. Phillies manager Gene Mauch argued and ordered his pitcher to go to his mouth on the next two warm-up pitches, which got both Mauch and Boozer ejected from the game and saw Mets shortstop Bud Harrelson step into the batter's box for the first pitch of the at bat with a 3–0 count, from pitcher Dick Hall, who replaced Boozer in the game.

Gaylord Perry, a member of the Baseball Hall of Fame with a 314–265 record, was suspended in 1982 for doctoring the ball.

On August 3, 1987, Joe Niekro was pitching for Minnesota against the Angels. After a particular pitch meandered toward home plate, umpire Tim Tschda saw an emery board fly out of Niekro's pocket. The pitcher was also carrying a piece of sandpaper that was contoured to fit a finger. He was suspended for ten games. But was he really guilty of cheating?

"The most amusing cheating episode I remember was when Joe Niekro, at the end of his career and pitching for the Twins, was asked to empty the back pockets of his uniform pants," recalls Larry Dierker. "When he did, a nail file came out, and he was kicked out of the game. I would bet that he forgot it was in there, because he always had a nail file with him. The knuckleball is a pitch that requires fingertip control. Joe was forever filing his nails to get them 'just right.' Think about it. If you had a nail file in your pocket, how would you take it out and scuff the ball without everyone in the ballpark seeing you do it? So, in effect, one of the few players who has ever been caught cheating was innocent!"

Just how a pitcher "loads" up the baseball with spit—or whatever substance he is using—can also be an entertaining exercise. Since a pitcher is not allowed to put his pitching hand to his mouth on the pitcher's mound—except for games played in cold temperatures, when the umpires allow them to blow on their hand—deception is the key. It has also increased the use of lubricant, which is typically hidden on the pitcher's uniform, the bill of his hat, or his glove—or even a Vitalis ball from a greasy head.

Pitchers such as Perry are renowned for their gyrations on the pitcher's mound, touching their uniform, their brow, the bill of their cap, the front of their uniform, all in an effort to either load up the ball with an illegal substance or to get the opposition so keen on catching them in the act that they lose their focus on the pitched ball.

The catcher can also help load the ball with a substance or cut it on his equipment, which is what Yankees receiver Elston Howard allegedly did for the great left-hander Whitey Ford. Emery boards are a popular utensil in the pitcher's arsenal as well. And after a strikeout or ground out, the third baseman can also load up the ball before he throws it back to the pitcher. A week after Niekro was suspended, Phillies pitcher Kevin Gross was also suspended for an incident involving sandpaper. In August 1987 an umpire found sandpaper glued to the right-hander's glove, earning him a ten-game respite. Gross, a solid big-league pitcher for fifteen seasons with the Philadelphia Phillies, Montreal Expos, Los Angeles Dodgers, Texas Rangers, and Anaheim Angels, sported a lifetime 142–158 record. His run-in with the laws of baseball was an example of a player just trying to hang in there.

"I suffered a herniated disc prior to spring training and spent the entire season in pain," Gross told Larry Shenk in "Catching Up with Kevin Gross," an article on the Philadelphia Phillies Web site. "There were times I could barely walk, but I wanted to keep on pitching. My velocity went from the low 90s to 83–84 m.p.h. I had heard of pitchers who tried it for maybe four or five games. My excuse is that I was trying to survive. I certainly knew better."

No matter what someone like the late, great Richie Ashburn might have thought, pitchers are not the only people on the baseball field that tried to gain an unfair advantage. In fact, Ashburn himself might have been the benefactor of some liberties taken that were over the line—the foul line. Groundskeepers in Shibe Park in Philadelphia, later known as Connie Mack Stadium, used to sculpt the third base line so that Ashburn, an outstanding bunter, could be assured that balls he bunted down the line would not go foul.

While the rules dictate certain dimensions of the playing field, such as the pitcher's mound and the distance between the bases, other variables can often be dictated by the groundskeepers. If a particular team has speedy players on its roster, the home stadium may have foul lines that are built up and sloped, ever so gently, making it harder for a bunted ball to roll foul, like at Shibe Park. But if a visiting team is coming to town that has a particularly fast runner who is an outstanding bunter, the club can make changes to ensure that bunted balls will roll foul. They can also make sure that the dirt cutout in front of home plate has hard dirt to make balls roll to the infielders, rather than die in front of the batter's box.

If the home team has a good base stealer, the groundskeepers can sculpt the area around first base to make it easier for him to get a good jump and good footing around the base. Conversely, if a visiting team sports a great runner, the area around first can be made soft, slippery, and muddy, making a good start off the base more difficult and spinning his wheels in the mud more prevalent. Remember: the grounds crew works for the home team.

It's not just pitchers who try to change their odds for success by doctoring the equipment. For every hurler going over that invisible line, there is probably a hitter doing pretty much the same thing. One of the ways hitters try to tip the scales in their own favor is by corking their bats—according to Matt Wood at Wood-Tang.com, "illegally doctoring a bat by drilling a hole in the barrel and filling it with cork or pieces of rubber." This is believed to help the ball fly farther. One of the most famous examples of bat corking was done by Norm Cash of the Detroit Tigers, who used a corked bat in 1961 when he led the American League with a .361 average with 41 home runs and 132 RBIs. He was a career .271 hitter who never hit higher than .286 in any of his other seventeen big-league seasons.

While Sammy Sosa has never been caught using illegal performance-enhancing drugs to date in his career, there was an instance where he was caught using a corked bat. The incident occurred in the first inning of a game at Wrigley Field on June 3, 2003, when his Chicago Cubs were taking on the Tampa Bay Devil Rays.

With runners at second and third, Sosa broke his bat hitting a ground ball to second base and was thrown out, supposedly driving in the Cubs' first run. But umpiring crew chief Tim McClelland met with his colleagues to examine the handle area of the bat, where they found cork.

After the game, Sosa was genuinely apologetic about the incident. "I use that bat for batting practice," he told a reporter with the Associated Press. "It's something that I take the blame for. It's a mistake. I know that. I feel sorry. I just apologize to everybody that are embarrassed. I use the bat for batting practice, just to put on a show for the fans. I like to make people happy and I do that in batting practice."

On July 15, 1994—nine years before the Sosa corking—a wild scene occurred in Chicago's old Comiskey Park. The Pale Hose and Indians were engaged in a tight race that year. White Sox skipper Gene Lamont, acting on a tip, asked the home-plate umpire to check for evidence of tampering in the bat of Cleveland slugger Albert Belle. The umpires saw nothing unusual in his bat, but they confiscated it, which was their right, locked it in the umpires' dressing room, and planned to send it to the league office in New York for an X-ray inspection.

During the game, Cleveland pitcher Jason Grimsley—the same Jason Grimsley who would later have a well-publicized, career-ending performance-enhancing drug situation—rushed to the support of his teammate. Grimsley reportedly went through an overhead crawl space and found the umpires' locker room where he switched Belle's corked bat with a legal bat belonging to Paul Sorrento. Why not simply replace the corked bat with another uncorked, legal Albert Belle model? Apparently, all of Belle's bats were corked.

The question most fans of all degrees of expertise wonder is: What advantage is there to the batter by using a corked bat? According to Wood, "Baseball lore says that hollowing out the wooden barrel and replacing it with lighter material allows the player to swing it faster and hit the ball harder. This alteration also supposedly makes the bat springier, catapulting the ball off the bat and sending it an extra 10–20 feet. In a game often decided by a fraction of an inch, this could mean the difference between a sacrifice fly and a three-run homer. . . .

"Baseball is a sport driven by the laws of velocity, acceleration, momentum, wind resistance, and friction. According to these laws, performing surgery on the barrel of a bat lends no improvement in performance, and it may even have an adverse effect. Corking a bat does reduce the weight of the bat, but no more than any other, legal methods. According to Robert Adair, author of *The Physics of Baseball*, there are much simpler, legal ways to achieve the same effects as corking a bat. You can choke up ¾ of an inch. You could saw off ¼ of an inch so you have a shorter bat, or you could put the bat in a lathe and take ¹⁄₁₆ of an inch off the barrel. This is legal. Players can also use bats that are hollowed out at the end of the barrel, producing a cupped shape. This legal alteration is also much more effective than cork, because it removes much more mass than boring a hole in the barrel and replacing it with cork or rubber.

"Swinging the same bat faster can help a batter hit the ball harder, but swinging a lighter bat faster doesn't necessarily improve performance. One of the basic laws of physics that affects a ball's flight, force, is a product of mass times acceleration. If a batter increases the rate of acceleration of a swing at the expense of reducing the mass of the bat, the net result can be the same as if he didn't do anything to change the bat."

One belief that continues to this day is that if a player gets a heavy bat and corks it, the better quality of the wood in the heavier bat will promote an advantage. The test results on this are still inconclusive.

"Hitters can get a little more power out of a corked bat," says Dierker. "Sometimes they use cork and sometimes they use something like chopped-up superballs. I think the extra power comes with the reduction of the weight of the bat. It is still just as hard, but it is lighter, which allows for a little more bat speed. I don't think that many—if any—players use corked bats these days. The bats that are commonly used now are already so light that they often explode into many pieces when they break. The heavier bats of bygone eras hardly never came completely apart."

Jim Evans agrees that corking a bat has limited benefit to the hitter. "Most physicists agree that the only advantage in corking a bat is the change in the weight of the bat and the bat speed," he says. "They do that legally now with the cupped bat that has the indentation in the barrel end. It's the legal way to lighten the bat and get more bat speed. Take an ounce or two out of the bat, and it's the increased bat speed that makes the ball go further, not what's in the bat. What the cork does is that it keeps the bat from breaking and keeps the integrity of the bat. It also won't have a hollow sound to it when you hit the ball."

So players continue to cork bats, even though there may not be a scientific reason to do so. Why? Simply because superstition plays a vitally important part in the game. If you think something makes you swing the bat better—even if it doesn't—why change? That belief may give you just the tiny advantage you need to play better.

While science can sometimes explain baseball, superstition is probably a more important element to understanding the game.

Science can explain or refute a phenomenon, but superstition and the general feeling that comes with a hitting or winning streak can trump science or even common sense. The game is chock-full of examples that show hitters going through an intricate collection of rituals before each pitch, while pitchers act out a seemingly unrelated routine of gyrations on the mound prior to uncorking the ball. If you think a particular behavior is contributing to a streak or a good performance, you don't mess with the behavior. This is why players grow beards during winning streaks, or don't have their uniforms laundered. No matter what, you don't mess with a streak—because in baseball, streaks are far and few between.

This concept was explained in the movie *Bull Durham*. In one of the most telling and entertaining scenes in the flick, veteran catcher Crash Davis tries to explain to baseball groupie Annie Savoy why she should not try to interfere with the belief of her boyfriend, pitcher Nook LaLoosh, who feels that his success on the playing field has a direct correlation to his lack of relations with Savoy in the bedroom. Davis reinforces LaLoosh's determination to stay out of Savoy's bed until his winning streak ends, which causes great acrimony between Davis and Savoy. As Davis explains to Savoy in the movie, "If you believe you're playing well because you're getting laid, or because you're not getting laid, or because you're wearing women's underwear, then you are. And you should know that."

Sometimes it's just that simple.

Another prevalent form of cheating in baseball is stealing signs. Now, not all sign stealing is illegal; in fact, stealing signs is a respected and honored art form that has been a part of baseball since the first sign was given. But, like everything else, baseball law and lore has its limits.

As mentioned earlier, if a batter peeks to see where the catcher is setting up before a pitch is thrown, he's not breaking any printed law of baseball. But if the catcher or pitcher notices that the batter snuck a look behind him, there's a good chance the next pitch will be in the general vicinity of his head. That's one of those unwritten rules of the game: Peekers never prosper.

But that doesn't keep them from trying. This is an ancient tactic that has been around for decades. In an article titled "How to Play Ball," which appeared in the *Washington Post* in 1909, the great Connie Mack explained, "Many batters watch the catcher closely to see what position he settles himself in before the ball is delivered." A sportswriter of the day advised a receiver, "You must guard against the batsman peeking back to catch his code. That is why the back stop stoops in calling for balls, by crouching he shuts out all possible vision of the batsman." That is unless, of course, a team uses a new and inventive way to steal signs from the catcher, such as in the 1950s, when the Chicago White Sox were accused of using a periscope from an old World War II submarine in the scoreboard to spy signs from the catcher.

That being said, many managers, coaches, and bench players try to increase their value to their team by stealing signs. They spend countless hours staring at opposing coaches and managers, trying to decode the meaning of a scratch, nose touch, or bill of the cap adjustment. Did you ever notice that whenever a runner advances from first to second base, ninety-nine out of one hundred times, the catcher visits the mound for a meeting with the pitcher? Are they deciding where to go for dinner after the game? Probably not. What they are doing is changing the sign sequence so that the runner at second can't watch the catcher signal the pitcher and try to give the batter a hint as to what's coming. In some of those meetings on the mound, the catcher and pitcher actually decide the entire pitch sequence of the at bat and then give insignificant signs that mean nothing—just to confuse the offense. Sometimes you get the impression that even the most sophisticated CIA operative would be lost on a baseball field.

Much has been written in recent years about speculation concerning the magnificent rally of the New York Giants, who overcame a 13.5-game deficit in August to steal the pennant from the Brooklyn Dodgers in 1951 when New York's Bobby Thompson hit "the shot heard 'round the world." Perhaps they *did* steal the pennant—by stealing opponents' signs. It seems that Giants coach Herman Franks would sit in the Giants clubhouse, which was located just past center field in the Polo Grounds, and read the signs the catcher was giving to the pitcher. He would then decipher the code and signal the dugout using a bell/buzzer system that would identify to the Giants the pitch that was about to be thrown; this information could then be relayed to the hitter. This type of electronic gadgetry is over the line according to the laws of baseball.

"To steal signs, you have to be an active participant in the game," says Evans. "We had a situation once where Oakland was using binoculars in the visiting bullpen in Kansas City, out in left field. All they had was a cyclone fence out there, and they saw the Oakland club trying to steal the catcher's signs. It was called to our attention and we went out there. By the time we got to the bullpen, the players had hidden the binoculars, but the fans told us where they were hidden. It's illegal for any nonparticipant in the game to use an outside aid like that.

"I don't think it helps that much. I've heard players say they don't want to know what pitch is coming. The oldest trick in the book is for the runner at second base to relay the signs to the hitter. He has a perfect view. That's why sometimes you see a wild pitch right after a runner gets on second base, because the pitcher forgets the change in the signs and crosses up the catcher.

"During the course of the game, any edge you can get is fine, as long as it's within the legal framework. Certain coaches can steal signs from the dugout. What a lot of fans don't realize is that the third-base coach is just a relay man. The actual sign is coming from the dugout as to whether you should hit, take, bunt, or hit and run. It's easier to steal the manager's sign than the third-base coach's sign because it's not nearly as sophisticated."

Just how true charges made against teams are and whether they ultimately gained any advantage from their alleged misdeeds will probably never be known for certain, but, true or not, they are far from the first instances of such practices in baseball. As historian and author Jerrold Casway wrote in his book *Ed Delahanty in the Emerald Age of Baseball*, such practices were part of the game for many years before Bobby Thompson's shot heard 'round the world.

"Every ball team sought ways to get the upper hand against its opponents," Casway reported. "The most successful ball clubs stole signs and looked for mannerisms that disclosed pitching tendencies. Once the signs were detected, it was only a matter of transmitting the information to a batter or baserunners. The Morgan Murphy System allegedly took this practice to a new turn-of-the-century technical height. Murphy, using binoculars, would steal the catcher's signs and relay the information on to a coach who passed it on to the batter. Murphy's innovation was that instead of a visual sign, he relayed the information by an electronic signal.

"Never more than a weak-hitting backup catcher, Murphy was a keen student of the game, wise to the idiosyncrasies of players and managers. He learned much about finagling from Charlie Comiskey, who managed him for three years in Cincinnati. Another one of Charlie's disciples was Tommy McCarthy, the league's 'sign detective.' It was said that McCarthy's system helped Frank Selee's Beaneaters with their pennants.

"For Murphy, this ability evolved into a role as a nonplaying bench coach, working with front-office man Billy Shettsline. Before long, Murphy moved to better vantage points, such as apartment or clubhouse windows, where he would steal the catcher's signs and use a newspaper, window shade or drapery to convey his message. Other teams attempted this tactic, but no one rivaled Murphy's skill or ingenuity.

"Former Philadelphia captain Bob Allen, the manager of Cincinnati, was alerted by Art Irwin to Murphy's new system. Allen was told that the Phillies had installed a box with an electronic vibrating buzzer under the third base coaching area with wires to Murphy's hiding place. Before a September 17 game, Allen visited Shettsline in the center field clubhouse looking unsuccessfully for the wires. When the game began, Cincinnati captain Tommy Corcoran started nosing around Pearce Chiles' third base coaching spot. By the third inning, Corcoran's 'scratching' alarmed Shettsline, Chiles, the groundskeeper and a police sergeant, who had all rushed to the digging site. Upon their arrival, Corcoran discovered and lifted a board, exposing a 'snuggly fitted electronic apparatus.' Players from both teams gawked at the hole, until umpire Tim Hurst ordered the game resumed.

"*Sporting Life* referred to Morgan Murphy as 'the Edison of base ball,' and most coverage of the discovery was humorous and damning. The league had no rule about stealing signs, and most teams at one time indulged in the practice. John McGraw confessed that one of his teams relayed stolen signs, and thanks to Dick Cooley, Pittsburgh awkwardly mimicked the Murphy system. But the sharp-eyed Morgan Murphy, an accomplished lip-reader, was one of a kind."

A full generation later, in the mid-1960s, Pittsburgh Pirates relief pitcher Elroy Face caused a stir when he was spied by Phillies manager Gene Mauch inside the scoreboard at Forbes Field in Pittsburgh. Mauch was certain that Face was stealing signs from the Phillies catcher and somehow relaying the information to his own batters. The forkball specialist tells another side of this interesting story.

"Once Gene Mauch had me thrown out of the scoreboard in Forbes Field because he said I was stealing signs," Face says. "But when I was there, the Phillies were hitting. So why would I want to steal our own signs? We used to go in there and smoke a cigarette and drink a pop or grab a bite to eat during the game. That's when we were on the left field line. When the other team was there, they could steal the signs. Gene Mauch's team was hitting when I was in the scoreboard. Why would I be stealing the signs from our team if his team was hitting?"

Why indeed? But whether or not Face was stealing signs from the scoreboard area, the story illustrates how the mere thought of the other team's gaining a tactical advantage can give an opposing team or manager a bad case of apoplexy.

"If players are cheating, they should be penalized for it," Face says. "You are supposed to go on your ability, not false ability. Even with corks in the bat, you still have to get the ball on the bat and they have to come together to make contact. Otherwise it's a pop-up. That is the most difficult thing to do in sports: Hit a round baseball with a round bat on the sweet spot.

"They accused me of throwing a spitball, of doctoring the ball, which I didn't do. Bill Rigney accused me of it. I wouldn't know how to do it. I guess guys did cheat, though, which was wrong. I don't think it should be done."

Of course, there are other things that happen in a game that fall outside of the rules but are accepted by the masses. Base running and plays around the bags are often brought into question. One of the most misunderstood plays in baseball occurs when a second baseman or shortstop fails to actually touch the bag on a force-out to begin a double play. Fans constantly argue that the "neighborhood" play is never called—except on those few occasions when it is called against their team.

While the rules may state one thing, the reality is that this play was originally intended to protect players from injury. And the reason you rarely, if ever, see a team complain about the play is that both teams want their players protected.

"That evolved through the years and is called the neighborhood play," says Jim Evans. "Umpires can call it any way that the management and the teams want it called. You can call it very strictly, or you can give the benefit of the doubt to help the players avoid injury. You allow them to get out of the way of the runner as long as the timing was good, if the throw beat the runner. If the throw takes the fielder off the bag, then the runner is safe. Both teams want it called that way. If you call a guy out who missed the base by a small margin, you will not get an argument. It was like an unwritten rule. Nowadays, with the replays and all the different camera angles, it's a little more difficult. But that doesn't give a real appreciation for what's going on in the field.

"Then you'll see base running where guys will go out of the base line at second base to screw up a throw to first. The runner's job is to take the fielder out, and there are legal and illegal ways to do that. It's legal if he can reach the base with any part of his body. That's fine, as opposed to following the thrower farther out. Another illegal slide is the roll block. Hal McRae took out Willie Randolph at second base on a roll block, like he learned playing football. The players will roll block the fielder from the knees down and knock him ass over teakettle and avoid the double play. The rule is that you have to hit the ground in the base path before you hit the player.

"The umpire has to interpret the rule book. So far I've identified 237 mistakes in the rule book. It is the intent of the rule that you have to act on. A runner trying to score from third base on a ball hit to the third baseman is smart to run in fair territory to make the throw tougher. Same as a runner going from first to second when the first baseman has to make the force throw. Running in the path of the throw is perfectly legal.

"Going to first, you have the runner's lane, which the runner is supposed to stay in, which I think is really antiquated. It's enforced differently than it was in the 1800s, where you had collisions at first base like you can at second, third, and home plate. In those days, the first base bag was half fair and half foul. Why wouldn't the runner just run over the first baseman? It would change the whole nature of the game. The runner's lane violation was to prevent the collisions at first base, not interference with the throw."

As the epitome of an impartial observer, the umpire has no interest in who wins the game. Rather, they are there to interpret and enforce the rules of baseball in a fair and impartial manner. But when it goes against your team, the umpire often takes on the characteristics of Darth Vader and the Evil Empire. It's a tough situation.

"People need to understand that umpires never try to make a call that will hurt a team," says Evans. "But it's the nature of the job. The job of the umpire is one of emotional detachment. That's something we need to train umpires. They come from the environment where they have been an active participant in the game and having a vested interest in who wins. As umpires, you become a third person that doesn't care who wins and loses. You have no emotional interest in the game. Being able to stand up and make a tough call that goes against the home team with fifty thousand fans screaming at you takes a special mental toughness. And it all comes with training."

While baseball has been damaged as much as any sport (with the possible exception of track and field) by the ongoing steroid scandals that have rocked the sports world, there is also a history of cheating that, while certainly wrong, could be considered a much more innocent way of skirting the rules. While the steroid situation is certainly not an acceptable form of cheating, many of the other ways of gaining an advantage during a baseball game are. In this day and age, a discussion of spitballs and corked bats seems a refreshing step back to a more innocent game.

5

FOOTBALL

Proceeding Illegally: Spygate, Stickum, Cheap Shots, & Recruiting

---

"I've always felt and decided to do things the right way and not try to gain an unfair advantage. We just try to follow the rules."

—Hays High School football coach Bob Shelton

"I think a lot has been made over this Spygate thing and I think they ought to throw it all out."

—Former NFL linebacker and coach Maxie Baughan

Some news stories never really leave the national spotlight. No matter how much time passes, our collective consciousness continually comes back to a specific incident, and we replay it time and again. In the time since revelations about Bill Belichick and the New England Patriots' Spygate scandal, the story has been reviewed as much as the Immaculate Reception of Franco Harris, when the Pittsburgh Steelers stole victory from the arms of defeat against the Oakland Raiders.

Are we to believe that New England is the only professional football team that bent or broke the rules in such a manner as Spygate? Is it that they were dumb enough to get caught that is the problem, or is there a segment of our society that roots against excellence and glories in their downfall? While there are many examples of cheating in football, ranging from the use of such substances such as Vasoline and Stickum to dirty play and recruiting violations in college athletics, a treatment of the Pats and taping needs to be addressed at least one more time.

It all started to come to light when it was announced that the National Football League had fined Belichick $500,000 and the Patriots $250,000 and a first-round draft choice in the 2008 draft for videotaping signals from the New York Jets in a game on September 9, 2007, in violation of NFL rules. In addition, the Patriots were required by the NFL to hand over all notes and tapes that dealt with the taping of opponents' defensive signals.

The NFL Game Operation Manual covers the practice of recording devices. In part, it says, "No video recording devices of any kind are permitted to be in use in the coaches' booth, on the field, or in the locker room during the game. All video shooting locations must be enclosed on all sides with a roof overhead." And, "Any communications or information-gathering equipment, other than Polaroid-type cameras or field telephones, shall be prohibited that might aid a team during the playing of a game."

What apparently happened was that the Patriots were filming defensive signals from an on-field location, which was clearly against league rules, and the Jets grabbed the camera that was being used to film the signals. The fines were levied against Belichick and the Patriots after a discussion with NFL Commissioner Roger Goodell. Belichick apologized to everyone who had been affected in a statement released two days later. He said that it was his understanding of the rules that it was legal to collect footage if it was not used during a game, but that he was sorry for his mistake in misinterpreting the rules.

"I know Bill Belichick well, and he knows better than to do that," says Maxie Baughan, who played ten years as a standout linebacker in the NFL with the Philadelphia Eagles, Los Angeles Rams, and Washington Redskins, earning Pro Bowl honors three times. He was also a defensive coordinator for the Baltimore Colts and Detroit Lions and coached with Tampa Bay and Baltimore. "Anything that you can do that's legal is not going over the line. I don't think this is going over the line. They never told us to not look at the signals from the other team. It was just normal. If you can't look at the signs, then you can't. But it's just normal. I think a lot has been made over this Spygate thing and I think they ought to throw it all out."

Baughan is either in the minority or part of a silent majority, because judging by the response to this story, Belichick, Patriots owner Bob Kraft, and all of New England were vilified as criminals to such a degree that their critics may also believe them culpable in the attack on the *Lusitania* as well as the assassination of Archduke Ferdinand that led to the start of World War I. The Pats organization has been accused of acting arrogantly, which will be left to the opinion of the reader, but the team's superiority on the football field cannot be denied. But nobody likes a smug bully, which many consider Belichick's team and the Patriots organization to be.

When news of the scandal broke, the Patriots were on their way to the first undefeated regular season since the 1972 Miami Dolphins, who captured football glory with a 17–0 record. The coach of that great Miami team, Don Shula, poured gasoline on the flames in November 2007.

"The Spygate thing has diminished what they've accomplished," Shula said. "You would hate to have that attached to your accomplishments. They've got it. I guess you got the same thing as putting an asterisk by Barry Bonds' home run record. I guess it will be noted that the Patriots were fined and a number-one draft choice was taken away during that year of accomplishment. The sad thing is Tom Brady looks so good, it doesn't look like he needs any help."

Are we to believe that the New England Patriots were the only football team taping opponents' signals in such a way? Hardly, it would seem. But shortly before the incident, the NFL sent a memo to all teams reiterating the league policy against taping in such a manner. The Patriots were caught red-handed—and they were caught red-handed just after receipt of the memo from the league.

But another issue continually comes to the forefront when any discussion of such dishonest behavior is undertaken. Obviously, Belichick and the Patriots broke a league rule by taping from the field. But in a more basic sense, is stealing hand signals cheating? Is it okay to have a sign-stealing guru on the sidelines or in the press box with binoculars so strong that it's possible to see the date on an opposing coach's watch, while filming the same signals and reviewing them is cheating? Are scouting reports a form of cheating? Even in high school football, you not only know a team's tendencies, but can steal audible signals at the line of scrimmage from the quarterback. For instance, if a team uses red as one of its hot colors, you knew which plays are to follow. Is that an unfair advantage, or is it just games-manship?

In his blog, O. C. Domer, Notre Dame alumnus Earl E. Baker pre-sented an interesting scenario dealing with questions about when cheating on the football field and on the sidelines actually begins. This entire idea sounds vaguely familiar to the Watergate hearings, with Sen. Howard Baker's omnipresent question: "What did the pres-ident know and when did he know it?"

"1. The coach yells from his sideline to his defense on the field, 'Two deep zone, blitz the strong side.' The offensive players hear the shouting and change their play.

"2. The coach yells the same thing from the sideline to his defense on the field, but does so in Spanish instead of English. The wide re-ceiver on that side of the formation understands Spanish and tells the QB what's going on, so he can call an audible.

"3. The coach has a white board and he writes on it in big letters, 'Two Deep Zone, blitz the strong side' and holds it over his head so his players on the field can read it. The opposing coach standing on his own sideline reads the white board and calls his play accordingly.

"4. Same scenario as 3, but the coach writes on the board '2D, BS.' The opposing coach cracks the code and figures out that '2D' is two deep and 'BS' is blitz strong, and makes his play call accordingly.

"5. Same scenario as 4, except the coach writes on the board, 'Bronco, Kangaroo.' The opposing coach doesn't crack the code dur-ing the game, but other coaches scouting the game from the stands are taking notes of the white board messages and the corresponding defenses being run. The following week that coach prepared his team to play based upon what he has learned about his opponents code system.

"6. Same scenario as 5, except that instead of a white board and code words, the coach signals his team with a series of odd hand sig-nals. Scouts in the stands take note of the signals and later, while watching game film, are able to figure out that when the opposing coach uses a slashing 'Z' signal the team runs an all-out blitz.

"7. Same scenario as 6, except instead of the scouts just taking notes, they actually have a mini-cam with them and record the sig-nals for use later when studying the game film.

"Apparently, the NFL has decided that scenario 7 is illegal under league rules. In my mind though, scenario 7 is not substantively different than the other scenarios. It's more sophisticated, but not substantively different. If a team is using a means of communicating play calls to its players that can be readily seen or heard by the opponent on the field or on the opposing sideline, then the opponent is entitled to try to break the code. It's up to the team using codes or signals to find a system that is secure. Like letting the linebacker call the play in the huddle. Or shuttling in the plays. Or using a wrist band with numbers that change every week (or even every half)."

Certainly, if the first six scenarios mentioned are okay by the NFL's morality standards, it seems strange that the seventh is not. The league—as well as many pundits and fans across the country—is seemingly making a federal case out of the situation. And, as noted in the preface of this work, a United States Senator, Arlen Specter of Pennsylvania, seems intent on doing just that. Lights, camera, . . . Senator!

After Goodell viewed the tapes pertaining to Spygate, he had them destroyed, which caused Specter, a ranking member of the Senate Judiciary Committee, to get involved in the situation. Apparently Specter thought that all the other unimportant matters of government could be put on hold to make sure that justice was being done in the NFL.

In a letter to Goodell, Specter said in part, "I am very concerned about the underlying facts on the taping, the reasons for the judgment on the limited penalties and, most of all, on the inexplicable destruction of the tapes." The two met in Washington, D.C., a week later, with Goodell insisting that he acted properly and had nothing to hide while Specter commented about the numerous questions left unanswered because of the destruction of the tapes.

Naturally, the Spygate situation led to other instances of other accusations against New England. In February 2008, the *Boston Herald*, citing an unnamed source, reported that the Patriots had videotaped the St. Louis Rams' workout on the day before Super Bowl XXXVI in New Orleans. A disgruntled former New England employee, Matt Walsh, who was fired following the 2002 season, said that he had much more information against the Patriots, but a confidentiality agreement he says he signed with the team kept him from commenting further.

These accounts raised such a furor that Willie Gary, a former safety with St. Louis, filed a $100 million lawsuit in New Orleans

District Court against the Patriots, Belichick, and Kraft, seeking compensation for the Rams' loss in the Super Bowl that year. Less than a month later, Gary and his attorneys withdrew the lawsuit.

In an interview conducted by the *Boston Globe*, Belichick said that taping practices was not something that his team had done, or something he condoned. "I have never authorized, or heard of, or even seen in any way, shape, or form any other team's walkthrough," he said. "We don't even film our own. In my entire coaching career, I have never filmed a walkthrough. I've never been on a staff that has filmed a walkthrough. I'm talking about when I was a head coach. As an assistant, I've never seen a head coach film a walkthrough the day before a game."

Belichick also said he felt that the term "Spygate" was unfortunate, because any taping the Patriots did was in plain view.

Stealing signs in any manner is beneficial only if a team has the ability to use the knowledge they garner. Many times, even if you know what is coming, you can't stop it. That's where talent comes in. Advance knowledge is not a guarantee of anything; all it does is prepare a team better. The team still has to execute.

"There was always the premise that George Halas had all the locker rooms bugged and that the locker room guys that picked up the towels were all his people," says Baughan. "They were supposed to be listening to everything that was said. This goes all the way back to when I started in 1960. Nothing was ever made of it. George Allen was accused of having scouts in the trees watching the Cowboys practice. One of them fell out and got hurt. I don't know for sure if he did it, but some people did some things. But mainly it's a joke, just like today it's a joke.

"Eight or nine years ago the coaches started to give signals on the sidelines. Everything they did, people watched to try to get some tips. It's been going on every since they started sending signals in. You'd try to mess them up by having two or three guys giving signs. You never knew which one was real. Too much of a big deal is made over something that has been going on for years and years.

"You would have the quarterback with a snap count of hut, hut, hut, and the defense would call out black, black, black to try to mimic the offense to draw them offside. The quarterback would call hard counts, snap his head forward, and move his foot. The defensive guys move toward the line to try to get the offense to move. It's a case of what you can get away with and what you can't, especially on the offensive line. What is holding and what is not? That's a debatable thing that could go on for years. No two officials see it alike. Just like pass interference.

"Look, I played thirteen years and coached for twenty years and I don't think you can steal signals and send something in. The defensive signal caller on the field can change the defense from the tendencies they see from the film work they did. If you prepare yourself, you know that down and distance equals plays that you have an idea are coming. That's football."

From the hysterical reaction to Spygate, you'd think it was the biggest scandal to have ever struck the National Football League. But an attempt to control the point spread of the 1946 championship game between the New York Giants and the Chicago Bears is potentially the NFL's version of the 1951 CCNY point-shaving scandal and the Black Sox scandal all rolled into one.

Prior to the big game, gambler Alvin J. Paris had offered Giants quarterback Frank Filchock and running back Merle Hapes upward of $2,500 each to help gamblers win a bet that Chicago would win by more than 10 points. The offer was discovered by a wiretap on the Paris's phone.

The day before the big game, December 14, 1946, both players met at the home of Bill O'Dwyer, the mayor of New York, where Hapes admitted being approached while Filchock denied any discussion about the point spread. NFL Commissioner Bert Bell announced that police had concluded that neither Filchock nor Hapes has taken any money or agreed to do anything but their best on the football field, and that the game would go on and that Frank Filchock would be allowed to play—but since Hapes admitted to being approached and failed to report the bribe offer, he would not be allowed to play.

"On the day of the championship game, Bell came with some people and picked us up," Hapes told author Dan E. Moldea in an interview for the book *Interference*. "They put us in a private room. We told them we were innocent, but their announcement had already been made. We had been blackballed and they had to do something. They didn't want to hear what we had to say.

"Sure I knew the man [Alvin Paris] and I couldn't lie about that. His father was a member of the Elks in New York and I was a member in Mississippi. The son asked me if I would throw the game and

I laughed at him. I said, 'I could never do anything like that. Forget about me.' Bell asked me if I took any money and I told him, 'I had nothing to do with it.'

"I still can't figure out why they didn't let me play. They let Frank play because they needed a quarterback. I was their sucker and I'm still damn bitter about it."

The Bears bested the Giants, 24–14, which represented a push—the gamblers neither win nor lost their bets. Filchock played nearly the entire game, completing nine of twenty-six passes for 128 yards and two touchdown passes, but he had six throws picked off.

Neither Filchock nor Hapes was found guilty of any wrongdoing, but their NFL careers were virtually ended. Filchock went on to play and coach in Canada and later played one game with the Baltimore Colts.

Cheating and bending the rules in football is not limited to the NFL. College athletes and even high school teams try to push that invisible line. Bob Shelton is the longest-tenured high school football coach in the state of Texas, where he has coached for forty-four years, forty of them at Hays High School in Buda, Texas. During that time, his teams have accumulated more than three hundred victories. He still recalls the first time an opponent cheated his team.

"The first time was in 1974 and we were playing Smithville High School in football," Shelton says. "We had won our first three games and were feeling pretty good about ourselves. But when we played them, it seemed like they just had us stopped. It was as if they knew exactly where we were going. They did. We were using walkie-talkies and they were on the same frequency listening to our plays. They knew what we were running before we even ran the plays.

"We didn't know it until the game was over. We got beat, 27–7. We felt like we had a good team, and then to get beat like that was really demoralizing. We ended up losing the game after that too. We let that game cause us to lose the next game as well. You have to know it's wrong. But sometimes coaches rationalize things. There is a lot of pressure that comes from within. It depends on the level. But people who are involved in athletics, whether they're players or coaches, are competitive by nature. People probably put more pressure on themselves just wanting to excel. And you always have outside pressure as well. Parents want you to win. They take it personally if you get beat.

Bob Shelton, famous Texas high school coach. Photo courtesy of Mary Stone.

"So you think that if there is an opportunity you take advantage of it. They probably looked at it as not going against the rules, even though they are. I've always felt and decided to do things the right way and not try to gain an unfair advantage. We just try to follow the rules.

"In high school ball, you are trying to lay the foundation for kids by what you teach them. If you cross the line, you are teaching them the wrong things. But when you get to certain levels, there is just so much pressure to win. And people don't care how you win. We're all trying to get an edge with weight training, or by the way you study films, or whatever. It's tough not to cross the line."

Players are instructed to protect their playbook with their lives. If your team's football bible were to fall into the hands of an upcoming opponent, that team's coaching staff would gleefully endure some sleepless nights in preparation for the upcoming contest, knowing full well what their opponent would be up to. Having a playbook is like having a full-course menu of a team's offensive and defensive schemes.

While it's possible to debate the seriousness of the various forms of cheating discussed in every sport, to the FBI, there was no doubt that former quarterback Karl Sweetan was up to no good in 1972. The eighteenth-round draft choice of the Detroit Lions in 1965, Sweetan had enjoyed some moments in the NFL sun. After replacing the injured Milt Plum at the helm of the Lions in 1966, he connected with Pat Studstill on a 99-yard touchdown pass against the Baltimore Colts, tying the league record. He threw ten scoring passes for the Lions the following year and spent three seasons as a backup signal caller with the New Orleans Saints in 1968 and the Los Angeles Rams in 1969 and 1970. He was let go by the Rams in September 1971.

But he resurfaced the following July when New Orleans coach J. D. Roberts reported to league security officials that Sweetan had contacted him to attempt to sell him the Rams' playbook. The league then notified the FBI, and Sweetan and his cousin, Wayne Boswell, were arrested and spent a night in jail, charged with wire fraud and interstate transportation of stolen property.

It was determined that the playbook had a monetary value of less than $5,000, which is the threshold for the sale of stolen objects across state lines to be considered a federal crime. As a result of that determination, Gerald Gallinghouse, the United States attorney in New Orleans, decided not to seek indictments.

Sweetan, who had hoped to return to the NFL, never did. He became a blackjack dealer in Las Vegas, where he died in July 2000 of complications related to vascular surgery.

Another way to get the lowdown on signals and tendencies deals with the transient nature of so many players and coaches in the league. It is easy to imagine that after the welcoming handshake a player receives from the coach of his new team, the staff interrogates him about the signs, play-calling tendencies, and other pertinent information from his former team.

A former player can alert his new team as to how the team audibalizes at the line of scrimmage, or can give a certain player's motion as a key that a particular play is coming. When coaches change teams—again, a regular happening in the NFL—the same type of research is done.

Maxie Baughan remembers how his Los Angeles Rams team took advantage of the Baltimore Colts.

"When I was with the Rams, we played against John Mackey of the Colts," he says. "They had some great teams in those years with Johnny Unitas. The split between Mackey's outside foot and the tackle would tell you if it was a run or a pass. That held up for years until somebody got traded and told him about it. You don't want to tell somebody how smart you are. You want to play dumb and use it game after game. George Allen would stay up all night watching film looking for tips."

There are also instances involving coaches who fear spies in their facilities and shred paperwork and other hints as to what a game plan might be—anything that could tip off an opponent as to what the team's sideline signal codes are.

Filming and taping were not the first rules incidents involving the New England Patriots, and certainly not the most inventive. What happens when a team does something so creative that it's not even against the rules yet? In fact, what about an occurrence that is so clearly deemed to be cheating that, after the fact, a league rule is made to outlaw it from ever happening again? Sounds like Hall of Fame stuff in the making. Such was the case during a game between the Pats and the Miami Dolphins on December 12, 1982.

Neither team had been able to score as the game was being played in a heavy snowstorm at Foxboro Stadium. After the Patriots moved the ball into scoring position, New England coach Ron Meyer had a stadium worker, Mark Henderson, who was on a prison work release program, drive his snowplow onto the field to clear the area where holder Matt Cavanaugh would spot the ball for kicker John Smith. The plow—er, ploy—worked, as Smith successfully booted a field goal that won the game and helped the Patriots make their first playoff appearance since 1979.

During the game, Henderson was at the controls of a John Deere Model 314 tractor with a sweeper attached. So even though this game is known as the Snowplow Game, that is a misnomer. It was on a tractor that Henderson was making repeated runs up and down the sidelines, making paths on every 10-yard marker from one side of the field to the other to enable the players, coaches, and fans to see where the ball was.

The Patriots were preparing to kick a field goal with 4:45 left in the fourth quarter from the Dolphins' 23-yard line. As Henderson drove the tractor to clear the 20-yard line, he swerved up to the 23, right where Cavanaugh was planning to spot the ball for Smith. With a clean Astroturf surface, Smith booted the 33-yard field goal through the uprights, earning a win for New England.

It should be noted that the broom and tractor made one last appearance at New England's final game at Foxboro Stadium in 2001. Mark Henderson, who had been released from prison in the 1980s, returned to a standing ovation when he drove the tractor and broom onto the field to reenact the 1982 clean sweep.

Another example of playing on the fence of legality in the NFL was Lester Hayes, a fine defensive back from the Oakland/Los Angeles Raiders. The five-time Pro Bowl player was known for the bump-and-run technique of defensive play and for using Stickum to such a degree that it was banned by the league.

The adhesive Stickum, along with other sticky substances such as glue, tree sap rosin, and certain food substances, was banned for play in the NFL in 1981 after Hayes used it to improve his grip on the football. This rule is known as the Lester Hayes Rule.

Hayes's former teammate, Hall of Fame receiver Fred Biletnikoff, must have been proud, for it was he who had introduced Hayes to the substance as a rookie. But Hayes was not just a player who used a foreign substance to attract the football. He was a master at the art of intimidation, which he had learned from his Raiders teammates Willie Brown, George Atkinson, and Jack Tatum. Hayes learned to hit opposing receivers in the throat when they crossed his path. While this illegal tactic drew penalties on numerous occasions, he also got in the heads of receivers, who may have concentrated more on him than on their pass routes.

Another Raiders Hall of Famer, offensive tackle Bob Brown, wore braces on his wrists. But what nobody knew was that the six-foot-four, 280-pounder had the braces made of a hard leather substance that slipped over his entire hand, including his knuckles. He became so expert at swinging his heavily weighted hands that he developed a pass-blocking technique that involved driving his fists into a pass rusher's chest.

Dirty players have always been a part of the game of football, as have cheap shots. But if a cheap shot is a determined effort by a team to injure and force an opposing player out of the game, it is a form of cheating. Two such instances occurred in 1989, in the two regular-season games between the Philadelphia Eagles and the Dallas Cowboys.

Bitter rivals for decades, the teams met on Thanksgiving Day, November 23, in Dallas. Philadelphia won that Turkey Day contest, 27–0, the only Thanksgiving shutout Dallas has ever endured. But it was a nasty game, filled with fierce hitting and scuffles between the players. Dallas kicker Luis Zendejas was forced out of the game with a concussion after being hit hard on a kickoff. Following the game, Jimmy Johnson, the Cowboys coach, accused Eagles coach Buddy Ryan of placing bounties on Zendejas, a former Eagle, and quarterback Troy Aikman.

The following month, the two teams played in Philadelphia on December 10, a contest that was also won by the Eagles, 20–10. It was a nasty, ill-tempered game on the playing field. But that rowdy exhibition was nothing compared to the behavior of Philadelphia fans, who threw snowballs, ice balls, batteries, and other objects at Dallas personnel. One game official was knocked to the ground after being pelted by snowballs. Johnson had to be escorted from the field by police, and Verne Lundquist and Terry Bradshaw had to dodge snowballs in the broadcasting booth. Even Ed Rendell, the future governor of Pennsylvania and an avid Eagles fan, admitted to being part of the troublesome crowd.

In the history of the NFL, there have been many dirty players. ESPN compiled a list of the dirtiest professional team players. Topping that list was offensive lineman Conrad Dobler, who played for the St. Louis Cardinals, New Orleans Saints, and Buffalo Bills from 1972 to 1981.

"I see defensive linemen jump to knock a pass down," Dobler said after he retired. "When that happened near me, I'd smack 'em in the solar plexus, and that got their hands down real quick. It's as if nobody wants to see anybody else get injured." Dobler punched Mean Joe Greene, kicked Merlin Olsen in the head, bit and gouged opponents, and once spat on an injured player, Bill Bradley of the Eagles.

Also on the ESPN list was another bad boy who affected games with his dirty play: Steve Wisniewsky, an offensive lineman with the Raiders from 1989 to 2001. He is considered by some to be the dirtiest player of all time because of his habit of chopping players from behind and going for the knees of opposing players.

Bill Romanowski, the hard-hitting linebacker who played with the San Francisco 49ers, Philadelphia Eagles, and Denver Broncos in his career, made a mockery of himself on *Monday Night Football* by spitting into the face of 49ers receiver J. J. Stokes. While that action certainly had no effect on a game, his shot that broke the jaw of Kerry Collins in 1997 was more substantive. In fact, he was fined $20,000 by the NFL.

One of the best defensive players in the history of the game, hard-hitting defensive back Johnny Sample, played for the Baltimore Colts, Pittsburgh Steelers, Washington Redskins, and New York Jets from 1958 to 1968. His autobiography, published in 1970, was titled *Confessions of a Dirty Ballplayer*. Former wide receiver Gene Washington says, "I played against Johnny Sample for the Colts, and nobody today plays the way he did. Playing on the line or over the line, as it relates to dirty tactics, there is not an equal."

Another member of the ESPN All-Dirty Team was the aforementioned Jack Tatum, who played with the Raiders and the Houston Oilers from 1971 to 1980. His book was called *They Call Me Assassin*. An extremely hard hitter, his aggressiveness during an exhibition game in 1978 paralyzed New England receiver Daryl Stingley, who died in 2007. Tatum was also fined by the league for a hit that sent Steelers receiver Lynn Swan to the hospital.

Cheating in football is hardly limited to the professional ranks. The same kinds of cheating are prevalent in the college game as well. On the subject of cheap-shot artists and plays: in October 2003 Ohio State linebacker Robert Reynolds knocked Wisconsin quarterback Jim Sorgi out of the game in the third quarter with a dirty hit. The ploy did not work, as the Badgers held on for a 17–10 win.

College coaches have long been known to send spies to an upcoming opponent's practice to try to get an unfair idea of what will be coming their way. Famous college coaches such as Darrell Royal of Texas, Barry Switzer of Oklahoma, and Frank Broyles of Arkansas, all good friends, talk with a twinkle in their eyes about instances of signal stealing when they coached against each other.

But perhaps the biggest violation of the rules in college ball has little to do with what occurs on the football field, although the end result can lead to a tremendous advantage in maintaining excellence on the field. One of the worst-kept secrets in collegiate athletics in general, and football in particular, remains recruiting violations. While the practice is not as obvious a measure of cheating as some of the other examples we've discussed, recruiting violations, kept unchecked, can profoundly affect a college football program, giving the school a tremendously unfair advantage in securing the services of some of the best high school recruits in the nation. With a wink and a nod, college fans and boosters often act as the go-between to grease the palms of young, often poor teens with a gridiron gift.

As far back as the 1950s, Bear Bryant's Texas A&M teams were placed on probation by the NCAA after he asked for the help of some well-to-do men in the oil industry to aid in the Aggies' recruiting season. The Southwest Conference was so ripe with corruption that seven of the nine schools were placed on probation in the 1980s. This list included Southern Methodist University, which actually stopped its football program for a year following a series of booster-related scandals school personnel were not only aware of, but in which they were also involved.

"I have not seen any recruiting violations personally," says Bob Shelton. "We see a lot of the college coaches who come by to see if you have somebody they want to recruit. The type of kids we have here, we don't have that many college players, and we've never had a pro player. The guys I've seen here recruiting have followed the rules. But that has not always been the case. Eric Dickerson was so highly recruited and there were a lot of rumors about schools giving him a car and things. There are lots of rumors of that type.

"When you have that one special athlete that everybody wants, sometimes things happen. Every coach in the Southwest Conference was watching Dickerson play. I've heard stories about coaches getting money for trying to influence the decision of what college their players will ultimately choose. That one special athlete, particularly in a sport like basketball, can get your program over the hump."

Even though the situation is held under much closer scrutiny than in the old days, payola passes hands and the system is bastardized. For every big-time scandal that hits the front page of the sports section, a mind-boggling number of incidents slip through the cracks. The money involved at this stage of the game makes this practice particularly hard to stop. And it's nothing new.

"There has been cheating in recruiting since recruiting began," says Maxie Baughan. "I went to Georgia Tech and I lived in Alabama. There were always stories about schools like Alabama,

Auburn, and Georgia getting in trouble. Alumni members or supporters would do things. There will always be people pointing their finger. The NCAA has done a good job of cutting down on it. But there is too much money involved now. Like that kid Reggie Bush from Southern Cal. They have been talking about the money his family got and the house and car and all this stuff. With all this money, it will not go away."

As recently as 2000, Logan Young paid a high school coach in Memphis $150,000 and a new SUV to help ink the signature of defensive lineman Albert Means. As a result, the Alabama football program ended up with five years' probation.

Troy Smith, a sophomore at Ohio State, was handed a two-game suspension for allegedly taking a $500 cash gift from a Buckeye booster in 2004. In 2006 Oklahoma quarterback Rhett Bomar and another player were kicked off the squad for receiving thousands of dollars while holding phony jobs at a car dealership with ties to the Sooners.

Maxie Baughan, former linebacker and coach. Photo by Tim McKinney.

Cheating in football is a different animal than it is in other sports, because in football, the degrees to which a team or an individual might go try to gain an edge are often within the law. Where it becomes cheating is when the effort goes over the line. And unlike the yard markers or the sidelines, the lines of the law are quite often difficult to discern.

But there is no doubt that players and coaches try to gain an advantage in football on literally every level, from the youth league teams through the high school, college, and the professional ranks. But Maxie Baughan relays a story about football great Jim Brown, who, in addition to being one of the most revered running backs in the history of the game, was also one of the best lacrosse players in college history and is a member of the National Lacrosse Hall of Fame. Brown was known to say that he'd rather play lacrosse six days a week and football on the seventh. And when you cause a rule change because of your play, you are taking it to the ultimate limit.

"Jim Brown caused the cradling rule in lacrosse," Baughan says. "He was the best lacrosse player that ever lived. He'd take the lacrosse ball and hold it in his chest and run up the field and knock everybody down. He was stronger and bigger and tougher than anyone. He was like a three or four time All-American in lacrosse at Syracuse. They had to change the rules and make it illegal to cradle the ball because of Jim Brown. Players make the rules."

And others try to break them.

6

HOCKEY

Slashing at the Rules

"When you get in a fight and lose, your teammates see it, twenty thousand fans see it, and then they replay it time and again on television on the highlights. So you embarrass yourself in front of a lot of people."

—Former NHL player Harvey Bennett

Hockey players are different. That's always been a belief among sports fans. Most reporters and journalists who cover multiple sports often say that hockey players are a throwback to a kinder, simpler time in athletics. They grew up skating and learning the game on makeshift ice rinks that their parents built behind their homes. Hockey was a family sport, played and enjoyed with relatives and neighbors. A highlight of the week was enjoying the Saturday night game on *Hockey Night in Canada.*

Hockey players remind us of our sports heroes of yesterday. While there are exceptions, of course, hockey players don't use the synthetic drugs so many athletes in other sports use and abuse in the new millennium. Hockey players like to congregate in the locker room, known as "The Room," or a local pub following a game to enjoy camaraderie over a few beers. In the best possible use of the word, many consider hockey players to be almost naive in this new and complicated world. They are straightforward, honest, and totally committed to their sport. Is there a more intense ninety seconds in all of sports than the typical shift of a hockey player? There is not, and that hell on ice demands giving your all. Players who don't won't last very long in the National Hockey League.

But while hockey players might be a throwback in many ways, that doesn't mean our hard-checking friends in the NHL and other hockey leagues don't try to get an edge on their competition. Because one of the greatest elements of hockey is just how much the players compete, literally risking life and limb for their team's success on every single shift. It's a fast game that mixes speed, skating, puck-handling ability, and bone-jarring hitting. Sometimes those bone-jarring hits may be over the line, and one of the most enjoyable elements of a hockey game is the game within the game, where players get away with everything they can get away with—and more.

But are hockey players dirty cheats who ignore the rules and play havoc with the way the game is supposed to be played?

"Hockey players are as dirty as players from other sports," says Harvey Bennett Jr., a center in the NHL who played parts of five seasons with the Pittsburgh Penguins, Washington Capitals, Philadelphia Flyers, Minnesota North Stars, and St. Louis Blues. "But do you consider it dirty, or is it just part of the game?

"There are plenty of examples of cheating, like when guys hold their opponents, hold their sticks, hit them on the back of their legs with a hockey stick to knock them off balance. Goalies have used cloth underneath their arms and netting between their legs to stop more pucks."

Each position on the ice has its own challenges, and the one-on-one physical battle only adds to the mystique and uniqueness of the game. The ultimate compliment a hockey player can get is to be said to be the kind of player who always wins a battle for the puck in the corner. But these battles for the puck can sometimes result in players dropping their gloves and fighting. While instances of fighting in the NHL are a mere fraction of what they were in the 1960s and 1970s, hockey is the only sport where participants are actually allowed to go toe-to-toe—except, of course, boxing. And there is an art to it. After all, when hockey players get into a fight, it's hard to remember sometimes that they are doing it on skates and on the ice.

"The big guys usually fight other big guys," says Bennett, whose brothers, Curt and Bill, also played in the NHL. "When fighting guys try to turn their opponents shirt. Phil Roberto used to twist the guy's shirt and tie up his arms. The most important thing in a fight is to get the first punch in. If you get the first one in, you have a massive advantage. You don't know who won or lost most of the time, except for who ended up on top.

"The first time I played against the Boston Bruins and Terry O'Reilly was playing for Boston, he and I got into a fight. You try to tie up a guy's right shoulder and have it in front so he can't come forward on you. The idea is to tie up his right arm so you don't get hit. So I got him and I'm hitting him, but I'm really getting hit too. Later in the locker room, I'm sitting next to Syl Apps. I was saying to Syl that I had O'Reilly's arm tied up and wondered how he was able to hit me. Syl just laughed and said, 'He's a lefty.'

"One of the best was Dave Schultz of the Flyers. He did a great job intimidating the other team. He and Bobby Kelly, Don Saleski, and Moose Dupont all did a good job. Guys did not want to go into Philadelphia to play. Schultz would come on the ice fresh at the beginning of a shift and his plan was to pick a fight with a guy on the other team at the end of his shift who was tired. Schultz was looking to win."

If a fight breaks out in a baseball game, it's a big deal. Often, a pitcher throws at a hitter, who takes offense and charges the mound. Both dugouts empty along, with the bullpens, and suspensions are no doubt handed out. If two basketball players get into it, the same result will be in the offing. But fighting has always been a part of the game of hockey. Fans enjoy it and the players realize that the chance to drop the gloves and get it on right then and right there probably alleviates a lot of dangerously dirty play with hockey sticks. But fighting is sometimes more than an action and a reaction by two players who are sick of each other. There are times in hockey when fighting is part of the game plan to give your team an advantage on the ice.

Fighting used to be a way for one team to gain an advantage that was more important than just winning the altercation. An overmatched team would often try to "trade" one of its lesser players, often a goon—hockey-speak for a tough guy with little ability—for one of the opposition's more talented players. If a good player gets into a fight with a goon and they both get five-minute major penalties, the goon's team wins the trade, because he won't be missed on the ice the way the better player will.

"That used to be a big part of the game in the '70s, getting the good guys off the ice," says Bennett. "The tough guys weren't as good, but they were big and strong. In the old days, guys would mysteriously get hurt or be sick when their team came in to Philadelphia or Boston. In Philly we called it the 'Flyers Flu.' You needed a big guy to keep the other team from running all over you."

Hockey players pay the price like few others, but they cheat, just like athletes from every other sport. The game is so fast that you sometimes have to look closely to catch it, or it can simply go unnoticed, like the ticking of a clock that you don't hear. Other times it is so blatant that it is obvious to everyone in the arena, with the possible exception of the player about to be penalized. But hockey players are as clever as they are dedicated. Much like in basketball, a big part of hockey is fooling the referees. One of the ways players always try to do that is by taking a dive.

Diving is a player's attempt to fool an official into believing he was either tripped or hooked by the stick of one of his opponents. Although referees can now penalize a player they believe is taking a dive, it has been and remains an art form in hockey.

"Billy Barber was the best diver in the world," says Bennett. "He looked like an Olympic gold medalist. The referees' knee-jerk reaction is to put their arm up and then it's too late to pull it back. They instituted a penalty for diving, and Billy was the template for it.

"The players all know that so they are very dramatic about the way they look. You have to remember, these guys have incredible balance and don't get knocked down that easy. The guys today should go to acting school, because the refs are calling diving penalties like crazy. But it's worth the effort, because power plays are a dominant part of the game. If you put the other team's skill guys out there on the ice with an advantage, they're going to beat you."

Another way hockey players cheat is by using stick blades with illegal curves. While every player uses a curved blad these days, hockey stick blades were not curved until the late 1950s, when Andy Bathgate of the New York Rangers began to experiment, bending the blade of his stick so it had a curve in it. He discovered that slap shots acted differently and erratically, making it more difficult for the goalie to stop the puck.

Then Stan Mikita and Bobby Hull saw the advantage of using a curved blade on their hockey sticks and asked their stick manufacturers to supply them with precurved blades. The bigger the curve, the crazier the puck reacted, and it got to the point where players like

Hull were using what became known as banana blades, with a curve as big as three inches. At this point in the game, most goalies still did not wear masks, and the erratic behavior of pucks shot with curved blades made life even more dangerous for netminders. As a result, the NHL began to limit the amount of curve that is acceptable on a stick. The legal limit today is three-quarters of an inch.

Players also use different kinds of curves for different results. A toe curve is concentrated near the toe of the blade and is favored by forwards who need to have better puck handling and accurate wrist shots. A heel curve is better for the big slap shots defenseman often take from the point.

The angle of the blade on a hockey stick is comparable to the difference between irons in golf. A more open blade, like a higher iron, means the face of the blade is turned more sharply, causing a higher trajectory than a closed blade face angle.

"The curve makes the puck dip and all kinds of other good stuff and you can shoot it harder," says Bennett. "I remember playing against Dennis Hull of Chicago when I was with Washington. Ronnie Low was our goalie. Hull would come down the wing and blow one right past the goalie's ear. Low came in and said, 'What the fuck was that?' Hull used to like to loosen up a goalie that way. In the old days, my dad was a goalie. When they had warm-ups before the game, if you shot a high one at your goalie, somebody would punch you, because you can really screw up a goalie that way. The warm-up is for them."

A player caught by the referees using an illegal stick receives a two-minute penalty. An opposing coach can call for a measurement of a player's stick—but he'd better be right, because his team will get a penalty if he's not. Players and coaches generally know which opposing players are using illegal sticks, but sometimes wait until a key moment in an important game to use that trump card.

Such was the case in game 2 of the 1993 Stanley Cup Finals between the Montreal Canadiens and the Los Angeles Kings. With the Habs down one game to none in the series, trailing the Kings, 2–1, late in the third period, Montreal coach Jacques Demers called for a measurement on the stick of Los Angeles defenseman Marty McSorley. His stick was found to be illegal and he received a minor penalty. Montreal's Eric Desjardins scored the tying goal on the power play and then lit the lamp again in overtime to give the Canadiens an important win. They went on to win the series—and the Stanley Cup—in five games.

"I don't believe in winning that way," Los Angeles coach Barry Melrose said following the game. The upstart Kings probably would have lost the series to the superior Montreal club, but Melrose, a hockey purist, no doubt felt that the game should be decided on the ice, rather than by the trump card the Canadiens used to help garner a victory.

While the three forwards and two defensemen on each team create the flow of the game, the last line of defense is the goaltender. While he doesn't need to skate, stickhandle very much, or check opponents into the boards, the goalie is responsible for keeping screaming, curving hockey pucks out of the net, often while being screened and otherwise interfered with and bothered by opposing players. There are also times when a goaltender's teammate is his worse enemy as well, when they block his view of an incoming shot traveling around 100 mph. There are also times when he is perfectly positioned, cutting down the shooting angle in such a manner that there is no way for the puck to go into the net—until, that is, it caroms off a stick or a part of the body of one of his well-meaning defensive teammates in front of the net.

All the protective equipment goalies wear represents a cornucopia of opportunity to bend the rules. For a number of years, teams have complained about Anaheim Ducks goalie Jean-Sebastien Giguere, suspicious that he uses illegal pads in the net. The complaints have centered around a portion of his leg pads that covers the five-hole—the gap between the netminder's legs—that open up when he flops down to block a shot. Any goalie caught using illegal equipment could be fined $25,000 and suspended for one game.

Some pretty good goalies from the past have gone over the line. Tony Esposito and Pete Peeters were caught with netting between their legs to help close that ever dangerous five-hole, and Ken Dryden was nailed for using leg pads that were too wide. Garth Snow had shoulder pads that resembled treehouses. If a goalie can increase his size in the net, there is less net to shoot at.

Hockey seems to be a sport with fewer examples of obvious cheating, partly because there are three officials on the ice policing the action. Curved sticks and illegal equipment notwithstanding, one of the best-known ways hockey players cheat is to take cheap shots at better players on the opposing team. There are countless examples of tough players gaining advantage for their teams this way, such as Eddie Shore's career-ending hit from behind on Ace Bailey and Marty McSorley's attack on tough guy Donald Brashear.

But because of the speed and flow of a hockey game, it's very possible for players to cheat on a thirty-second shift on the ice and not be whistled down by the officials. Hockey players may be arguably the best athletes in sports, because when they are on the ice, they are usually going at full speed the entire time. When they are outclassed as far as talent and ability is concerned, dirty and illegal plays can often be the great equalizers.

Another area of contention is that when a cheap shot occurs, quite often it is the player who retaliates who is penalized. The good teams normally have players who wait for an opportunity to respond when it won't penalize their club. Former Chicago, Philadelphia, and Pittsburgh defenseman Ed Van Impe was often quoted as saying that it is a long career, meaning there will be many opportunities in the future to get revenge on a player who may have gotten an initial advantage.

7

BASKETBALL

In the Penalty
with Official Incompetence

"They should hire you, train you, and hold your ass accountable. But it's a flawed system."

—Former NBA official Mike Mathis

The 2007 scandal involving former National Basketball Association referee Tim Donaghy is just the latest of a long litany of point-shaving conspiracies and gambling connections that have rocked both professional and college basketball. An NBA referee for thirteen years, Donaghy officiated 772 regular-season games and 20 playoff games. The Villanova University graduate resigned from the NBA on July 9, 2007, amid reports from the FBI that he bet on games he officiated during his final two seasons, making calls that affected the point spread in those games.

Point shaving normally occurs in amateur and collegiate athletics, where uncompensated athletes are more vulnerable to a gambler's money. But the Donaghy gambling revelations sent out shock waves that resonated throughout professional basketball. Less than two weeks after Donaghy's resignation from the NBA, *New York Post* columnist Murray Weiss reported on the FBI investigation into allegations that an NBA referee had bet on games in which he could control the point spread. It was later revealed that Donaghy, who has a gambling problem, had places tens of thousands of dollars in bets on games during the 2005–2006 season and had been approached to work on a gambling scheme by mob associates.

Donaghy appeared in federal court in Brooklyn on August 15, pleading guilty to conspiracy to engage in wire fraud and transmitting wagering information through interstate commerce. He told U.S. District Judge Carol Bagley Amon that he used coded language to tip off his friends James Battista and James Martino about things like the physical condition of players and relations between players and referees.

He and his coconspirators used a code involving the names of Martino's brothers. If Donaghy mentioned his brother Chuck, who lived in the Philadelphia area, they should bet on the home team. But if he mentioned Martino's brother Johnny, who lived outside of that area, they should pick the visiting team.

For disclosing such information, he initially received $2,000 per correct pick, until his picks proved to be so accurate that Battista increased his take to $5,000 per pick. In total, he received approximately $30,000 for passing along information to bookies.

"Our rules are clear that referees may not either gamble on our games or provide information to anyone about those games," says NBA Commissioner David Stern. "We educated our referees intensely. We have training camp presentations, we have brochures, we distribute work rules, they are visited by security, and we give them copies of compliance plans and the like that make it clear that not only aren't they permitted to either gamble or provide information to people, but they may not even provide other than to their immediate family the details of their travel schedules or the game they are going to work."

Donaghy was fined $500,000 and will also have to pay at least $30,000 in restitution. On July 29, 2008, he was sentenced to fifteen months in prison.

While awaiting sentencing, in what appeared to be a last-ditch effort to get leniency from the judge, Donaghy exaggerated his cooperation in the gambling investigation, according to prosecutors. Then he alleged that there were other referees who took direction from league executives about not calling technical fouls on certain star players, to avoid hurting ticket sales and television ratings. He charged that some officials accepted free merchandise and socialized with players and coaches, which compromised their integrity.

He also said that officials assigned to work the 2002 Western Conference Finals between the Sacramento Kings and the Los Angeles Lakers helped force a seventh game by favoring the Lakers in game 6. He called the referees in question "good company men" who made up fouls against Sacramento while choosing to ignore Laker fouls.

Stern says that Donaghy's claims were false and that he was "singing" to help get a lighter sentence. In a related story, the U.S. Attorney's Office announced that it would take no action based on Donaghy's charges.

"I have been involved with refereeing and obviously been involved with the NBA for forty years in some shape or form," says Stern. "I can tell you that this is the most serious situation and worst situation that I have ever experienced either as a fan of the NBA, a lawyer for the NBA, or a commissioner of the NBA. And we take our obligation to our fans in this matter very, very seriously."

The realization that one of their officials was involved in such a fantastic plot could have been the NBA's Waterloo. But at least one former NBA official, referee Mike Mathis, feels that the game has come to a point where the officials and their supervisors should come under much greater scrutiny. An NBA referee for twenty-six years. Mathis officiated nearly 2,340 games, 12 NBA Finals, and three All-Star Games. Since his retirement in 2001, he has been involved in ProHoops Courts Inc., which specializes in the installation of basketball goal systems and playing surfaces. But his interest in the betterment of the game he loves is never far from the surface.

"In terms of the end product you see today, games are mismanaged and games are misofficiated," Mathis says. "Everybody is not 100 percent accurate. The fallacy in the officiating ranks right now is that they say they get it right 90 to 95 percent of the time. That's not true. That's far from true. There is a basic problem with officiating.

"My idea of officiating is not going out on the floor and trying to make friends with the players. My idea is to treat the twelfth guy on the bench as well as you do Michael Jordan. That's not always the case with all referees. They all want to be loved. If you are getting good vibes from a player, it's to get the next call, not to become the referee's best friend. The players try to use the officials and it goes on

24/7. You can watch how coaches work officials, and to me, that's not how you should do it. You don't get friendships from a game; you gain the respect of the players, coaches, and fans by treating everyone the same and making it a level playing field.

"There are three flaws in the system. Number one, you hire good people. Then, when you have good people, you teach and train them. And third, you hold people accountable for what you teach them. It's no different than a good business plan. Look at Tim Donaghy. He had a history of attacking neighbors and putting dead animals in cars. How did he ever get hired in the first place? A lot of officials come from the Philadelphia area. Ed Rush, the supervisor of officials, was from Philly. The good old boy system is alive and well in the NBA.

"The teachers and trainers of officials are people who got fired by the NBA. Officials are causing the wrong teams to win. It's not cheating by the referees. The league is cheating the fans and the game by not having the right people out there. Instead of guys who were fired by the league, or who worked two playoff games in twenty-eight years, why don't they have guys who worked and did a good job for thirty years?

"Holding guys accountable is basically nonexistent. That's what happened in the Tim Donaghy case. Things kept popping up. The FBI told me in an interview that gamblers only care about how their bet goes, not who wins or loses. Donaghy was a crew chief. My career lasted twenty-six years, and what people think about a referee now is a whole lot different than before. The FBI told me that his crew led the entire league by far in the number of fouls called. He, as an individual, led everyone in the league in the number of fouls called. In seventeen straight games he officiated, the over number hit.

"They should hire you, train you, and hold your ass accountable. But it's a flawed system."

The inference is clear. The best way to beat the over number—the gambling high number for points scored in a particular game—is from the foul line. The more points that are scored when the clock is not moving, the better the chance even more points will be scored later. An official does not have to affect the ultimate outcome of a game to work in concert with elements of society that should not be involved in the game. All he has to do is call a ton of penalties and line his pockets as the over number is exceeded, earning gamblers a huge payday.

When it comes to basketball, it's not all about shaving points or affecting the over/under for profit. That is a sinister bastardization of the game. Cheating in basketball is a much more subtle exercise made by graceful, talented giants who not only hide their deviations from the rules, but often attempt to place blame on their opponent. Basketball is a game to be enjoyed on many different levels, but a study of the intricate ways in which the players attempt to skirt the rules brings forward a whole new level of interest.

We've often heard the refrain that in football, the officials could literally call a penalty on each and every play. The same could probably be said of each jaunt up and down the court. Unlike football, where interior linemen have a more hidden war in which all sorts of gridiron atrocities are committed, basketball players are much easier to see as they try to gain an advantage over their opponents.

As players mature through neighborhood games, high school, college, and then at the professional level, their expertise at bending the rules matures along with them. And along with hockey—where a player can attempt to draw a penalty by taking a dive—basketball is one of the few sports in which an athlete can try to get an opponent penalized for his own actions—or if the player knows almost for certain that committing a certain foul at a certain time will not result in a call by the referee.

"The veterans know how to play the game," says Mathis. "You'll see guys cold-cock a guy at the end of a quarter or the end of the game. The refs won't call it. But if it's a foul during the first minute of the game, then why isn't it a foul in the last minute of the game? To me, it is."

Part of the maturation process in any basketball player is the ability to act outside the rules in a way that is not obvious to the officials. Most referees are savvy enough to know the difference between a feigned fall or an insignificant push and an actual foul. It is through experience that players learn the difference as well. There are countless examples of falls, pulling an arm, grabbing a jersey, setting illegal picks, and the well-placed hand or elbow that can be hidden by a wily veteran that a younger player might not be able to camouflage quite as well.

Did a player illegally bump into the opponent in front of him in an attempt to get to a loose ball, or did the player in front stop short and fall forward to get a call? There are so many examples of calls that could go either way during the course of a game that the officiating crew can become key players in the outcome of a game. And what fans and players alike hate to see is an officiating call decide the ultimate outcome.

"At the end of the game, you call it the same way you did during the game," says Mathis. "You call it the same way in the playoffs as you did in the regular season. They didn't give me a separate rule book for the last minute of the game, or for the playoffs. I call it the same way I did during the regular season. Let the players decide the game. Why should the playoffs be reffed any differently? But they are. The reason given is that the players get more intense, so officials let more go. Refs don't have the intestinal fortitude to call the game the same way.

"But if you don't call anything, you are letting the players call the game illegally. How many times have you seen a guy take a long desperation shot at the end of a quarter and the guy gets tackled? Nothing is ever called. If he is fouled in the act of shooting before the horn goes off, it should be a foul.

"It has evolved to a point where I've had teams hire me as a consultant because it's obvious that the NBA doesn't care to do anything about their system. So I've been hired by some teams to teach their players reality officiating. Here is the rule book and here is what is called. It says a foul is a foul, but I teach my players to foul at the end of the quarters or the end of the game because the referees don't have the balls to call it. On a free throw, push the guy in the second space under the net. It's a foul, but guys don't call it. So I teach guys on the second lane space to push their guy under the basket, and 99 percent of the time it won't be called.

"There are so many tricks. I've got a list of about thirty plays that I teach teams—all the things that players use to try to trick the refs. Flopping is one. Carrying the ball is another. How the little guy drives the net, jumps into the big guy, and the big guy gets the foul. It has been allowed to get to this point because it's been accepted.

"Just look at the refs today as compared to twenty years ago. It looks like there are a bunch of bodybuilders out there. Look, if the league wants to hire a bunch of pretty boys, that's fine. But they have no balls between their legs. I want a guy with balls who can referee. Don't give me a guy with good looks who has no balls. Those transplants don't work."

Not surprisingly, the NBA is of the opinion that its referees are right much more than they're wrong and that the checking systems in place are effective.

"By and large they get it right most of the time," says Stern. "They get it wrong sometimes. Sometimes they perhaps carry themselves in a way that is not as modest as we would prefer, but they do their darnedest to get the result right. And frankly, I'm more concerned, rather than chastising them, with reassuring them that I am committed to protecting them while at the same time making sure that we keep our covenant with our fans.

"On the court we have, since the beginning of the 2003–2004 season, been implementing a system that is designed to capture every call that a referee makes and every noncall that is deemed by observers to be incorrect. We have retained thirty observers, one at each of our teams' games. They are, in effect, charting the game with respect to the calls and other observations that they make. They then review the game on tape. This system was designed for their development, to make them better officials, to increase their call accuracy, and generally to improve the quality of their work."

Mathis has had the pleasure of officiating games featuring some of the greatest stars of the game like Julius Erving, Michael Jordan, Larry Bird, and Charles Barkley. Not all of the interaction has been pleasant.

"I lived through Dr. J, Larry Bird, and Michael," he says. "I saw some of the great ones. Just get their respect and move on. You get their respect by treating them all the same. Me and Barkley never got along. He hated me. Why? Because he wanted special favors. He still hates me. I threw him out of games ten times one season. I threw him out once when he was shooting free throws.

"I called a technical foul on Michael Jordan one night in Seattle. He said to me, 'C'mon Mike, nobody calls that shit on me.' That was a great compliment. But I had the balls to make the call."

As noted earlier, some of the gamesmanship in basketball has nothing to do with point shaving and favoring the better players to increase attendance and television ratings. Many players on all different levels try to master the art of what Mathis calls "fooling the referee." And this practice goes on in schoolyards, high schools, and colleges as well as in NBA games. It's the game within the game.

There is a long history of one-upmanship in the college game. Some of it comes into play before the contest itself begins. Numerous colleges have been known to put out the hot carpet for their opponents, heating the visiting locker room to the point where the players are exhausted before even taking the court. At one point in the 1980s, when visiting Maryland's Cole Field House, the Duke squad often dressed in the hallway outside the locker room and tried to pry open the back windows.

Other schools, like Cincinnati, Clemson, and Oregon, often situate the visiting locker room far away from the court, which, in effect, shortens the visiting team's halftime break. At Clemson, visiting teams had to go up a tunnel, take an elevator, and walk a long distance to their locker room. By the time they got to the room, it was pretty much time to turn around and go back to the court.

At some Southeastern Conference schools, during the visiting team's shootaround the night before a game, the gym is dimly lit so that the players have trouble seeing and the coaches find it difficult to read their notes. Auburn has been accused of taking air out of the balls before their opponents' shootarounds. While these practices aren't against the rules, they can antagonize an opponent and get them off their game mentally.

There was a time when East Tennessee State and Chattanooga didn't bother to close their gyms during their opponents' practices, allowing students to run around and be a distraction on the court. Of course, the best revenge for the school is to ignore the shenanigans and just play their best and win the game. But the home team will often try to do whatever it can to stack the cards against the visitors. It might work and it might not, but doing anything to get their minds off of the task at hand has got to be considered an advantage. And that's what athletes in every sport are trying to gain—an advantage.

8

TARNISHED GOLD

Olympic and Amateur Athletic Cheating

"The Games today are the greatest celebration of humanity, an event of joy and optimism to which the whole world is invited to compete peacefully. Every four years, humanity celebrates, embraces and honors sport, and the world realizes the Olympic ideals of culture and peace."

—The Creed of Olympic Honor

Olympic organizers have packaged the games in such a way to suggest that the gathering of the world's best amateur athletes every four years is the purest form of sport. Here is a venue in which all the countries of the world put down their weapons and compete for glory and pride on an equal playing field. One cannot argue the sentiment, or the effort to create and maintain a haven of sports.

In the three-thousand-year history of the Olympics, there certainly has been an impressive array of stellar athletes who have done the ancient tradition proud. The history of the games is replete with wonderful stories that illustrate the best human traits of competition and courage. One of the earliest Olympic heroes was a wrestler named Arrhichion, who actually fought to his death in 564 BC. He was caught in a lethal ladder hold and was dying from asphyxiation. Inspired by a shout from his coach, he was able to roll over and give his opponent's foot a savage twist. The opponent raised his finger to surrender the match just as Arrhichion died.

The whole idea of laying down arms, putting petty and serious issues aside, to compete on fields of athletics is best summarized by an excerpt from the Olympic Web site. In part, the Creed of Olympic Honor says: "In the ancient Olympic Games, a truce was declared so that what is good and ennobling in humankind would prevail. The Games today are the greatest celebration of humanity, an event of joy and optimism to which the whole world is invited to compete peacefully. Every four years, humanity celebrates, embraces and honors sport, and the world realizes the Olympic ideals of culture and peace."

Tens of thousands of spectators would line hillsides to view the ancient games. Before the start of the games, the athletes would march through a collection of statues of gods and watch as oxen and boar were sacrificed at a forty-foot statue of Zeus. That makes the Olympic Torch seem rather tame by comparison.

Much like today, the athletes of those ancient times were looked at as heroes and treated accordingly. They were showered with fame and prizes. The winner of the boys' station race at the Panathenaea at Athens received a supply of olive oil worth the equivalent of $45,000. They also received annual salaries and other perks of the day, including free food, complimentary seats at entertainment events, hometown parades, statues in their honor, and sex partners.

Conversely, those who did not win in the games were subject to disgrace by their coaches. As the Greek poet Pindar wrote, losers would "slink through the back alleys to their mothers."

In ancient times, the games lasted for five days. Some of the events from those early games are part of the modern Olympics, including discus, javelin, running, wrestling, and boxing. Events such as the mule cart race, contests for heralds and trumpeters, and even poetry reading—included in the games thanks to a bribe by Roman emperor Nero in AD 67—have fallen by the wayside. In fact, in that year's Olympiad, Nero paid off the council judges who oversaw the games to hold events out of sequence, in a year they were not scheduled, so he could compete and win. Nero received the equivalent of six gold medals that year.

But, of course, cheating in the ancient Olympics and, indeed, the idea of any kind of behavior to give an athlete an unfair advantage over his competition in these hallowed games is ludicrous, isn't it?

Well, apparently not. While the three-thousand-year history of the games is filled with classic athletic achievement, in ancient times the games were tainted by the same problems we see today, such as cheating, bribery, gambling, and other such undesirable behavior.

The earliest incident of cheating happened in 388 BC, when Eupolus, a boxer from Thessaly, bribed three opponents to take a dive. This is considered by many historians as the first recorded act of cheating in sports. Performance-enhancing drugs may not have been part of the sports landscape in days long ago, but there are a plethora of examples of ancient athletes trying to gain an edge. For instance, Greek athletes drank wine potions, used hallucinogens, and ate animal hearts and testicles to become better athletes. They also gorged themselves on meat, which was not a huge part of the Greek diet.

Athletes were also known to consult fortune-tellers and magicians in search of victory potions. They also had curses put on their opponents so they would fail.

Even the origins of the games themselves are mired in fables of legend as well as deceit. One of the myths involves the hero Heracles, who won a race at Olympia and then decreed that the race should be reenacted every four years. Another myth claims that King Iphitos of Elis, who consulted the Pythia, the oracle of Delphi, to try to save his people from war in the ninth century BC, was advised by the prophetess to organize games in honor of the gods. Iphitos's Spartan adversary then decided to stop the war during the games, which were called Olympics, after Mount Olympus, the mountain on which the Greek gods were said to live.

Then there is the story of a young Greek charioteer named Pelops. King Oenomaus had challenged the suitors of his daughter Hippodamia to a race, under the pain of killing the loser. Pelops, the fourteenth suitor, received help from his old lover, Poseidon, who provided him with divine horses and chariot. Pelops then bribed Oenomaus's charioteer, Myrtilus, who switched the linchpins from Oenomaus's chariot with pins made of beeswax. As a result, the linchpins melted during the race and Oenomaus was killed. Pelops married the princess. He also murdered Myrtilus. To celebrate his victory, Pelops established the Olympic Games.

One of the great endurance competitions in all of sport is the marathon. This race pits world-class athletes against each other as well as themselves. Early on, the length of the marathon was not fixed. All that mattered was that all runners competed on the same course. So while the length of the race was always similar, it varied in length depending on the route established by each venue. Of the first seven Olympic marathons, six had different distances.

Finally, in 1921, the International Amateur Athletic Federation decided that the official marathon distance would be 26 miles, 385 yards. But no matter the exact distance, this event has represented yet another opportunity for athletes to attempt to cheat. With the length of the event, there are numerous places during a marathon race where someone could sneak onto the course during the actual race and try to steal glory at the end.

Such was the case in April 1980, when a Cuban American runner named Rosie Ruiz Vivas appeared to be the first-place female competitor in the eighty-fourth Boston Marathon, with a record time of 2:31:56.

Race officials began to suspect that something suspicious was up almost immediately, as no one could remember having seen her during the race. Some members of the crowd watching the event revealed that they had seen her jump into the race during the last half mile. She then sprinted to the finish line.

Race officials eventually stripped Ruiz of her Boston Marathon title, awarding top honors to Jacqueline Gareau of Montreal, who finished with a time of 2:34:28. It was later discovered that Ruiz also had cheated in the New York City Marathon, which had qualified her to run in Boston. She had apparently traversed part of the course on the subway.

But Ruiz was neither the first nor the last runner to cheat during a marathon.

The 1904 Olympic marathon was held on an oppressively hot day in St. Louis, which precluded more than half of the thirty-one starters from finishing the event. Fred Lorz crossed the finish line far ahead of his nearest competitor, with a time of 3:13. He had already broken the tape, posed for pictures, and had a floral wreath placed on his head by Alice Roosevelt, the daughter of President Theodore Roosevelt, when, amid suggestions by some spectators that he may not have run the entire race, Lorz admitted that he had cheated. He had suffered from cramps early in the race, and at the nine-mile mark he got into the car of an official, who drove him the next eleven miles of the race, from which point he decided to run into the stadium and break the winner's tape as a joke.

The humor of the situation was lost on Olympic officials, who suspended him from any future amateur competition, although he was later reinstated and went on to win the Boston Marathon in 1905.

The gold medal was then awarded to Thomas Hicks, who, it turned out, was not exactly squeaky-clean either. His time of 3:28:58 was the worst Olympic marathon-winning time in the history of the event. Hicks's unsavory claim to fame is that he was the first Olympian to take performance-enhancing drugs; his trainer gave him strychnine and egg whites as a stimulant to keep him going in the heat.

Just how slow was the field in St. Louis in 1904? A Cuban postman named Felix Carvajal ran the race in street clothes, took a break, and ate some apples at an orchard. He then got sick from eating what was rotten fruit, took a rest, and rejoined the race. He finished fourth.

In 1991 there was more deceit afoot at the Brussels Marathon. The apparent winner of the marathon, Abbes Tehami, had lost weight during the race—not unusual for a marathon runner, but he had lost quite a bit more than would be considered usual. Even stranger, he also lost the mustache that he had begun the race with.

It seems that the mustachioed runner who started wearing bib number 62 was, in fact, Tehami's coach, Bensalem Hamiani. A little over seven miles into the event, Hamiani veered off into the woods and gave the bib to the clean-shaven Tehami.

Organizers didn't split any hairs over the matter; they awarded the top prize to Soviet runner Anatoly Karipanov, who had a winning time of 2:18:04.

Cheating is not limited to Olympic and running events, as evidenced by the quarterfinals of the 1986 World Cup, when Argentine star Diego Maradona scored a goal with his hand. After scoring the goal, he told his teammates to embrace him or the referee might not allow it. The referee did not see it, and, despite pointed protests from their English opponents, the goal was allowed to stand, which helped Argentina go on to win the game, 2–1, on its way to winning the World Cup. Maradona described the goal as "a little with the head of Maradona and a little with the hand of God. The goal became known as *la mano de Dios*, or "the Hand of God."

It should be noted that Maradona, one of the finest players of his era, also scored the second goal of that game, in which there was no controversy, simply awe. He picked up the ball in his own half of the field, and with eleven touches, he eluded defenders and ran more than half the length of the field, dribbling past five English players— Glenn Hoddle, Peter Reid, Kenny Sansom, Terry Butcher, and Terry Fenwick—before scoring past goalkeeper Peter Shilton.

It took until 2008, but Maradona eventually admitted that he punched the ball and apologized to English fans. "An English supporter came up to me this weekend, asked me for an autograph, and said, 'You are a legend,'" Maradona told the *Sun*, a London newspaper, during a trip to England. "This made me very happy. Your people are so polite and kind despite the history between our countries. If I could apologize and go back and change history I would. But the goal is still a goal, Argentina became world champions and I was the best player in the world. I cannot change history. All I can do now is move on."

Cheating and skullduggery have even been seen in one of the most enjoyable Olympic sports for both men and women: figure skating. The United States has a long, proud tradition of Olympic success in the sport. But as in every other sport where judges are involved, the participants try to do everything in their power to gain an advantage.

Leading up to the 1994 Olympics in Lillehammer, America's brightest hope for a medal was a polished, attractive skater named Nancy Kerrigan, who seemed to have a real shot at the gold medal. One of her top competitors in the United States was Tonya Harding, an athletic but undisciplined performer. For all of Kerrigan's charm, Harding appeared rough around the edges and a little wanting in the feminine and ladylike traits characteristic of the long line of American medal winners before her.

As the 1994 games neared, Harding and her then-husband, Jeff Gillooly, hatched a plan that could lead the way for her to capture a medal. (It should be noted that Harding has always maintained her innocence and asserted that she only learned about the plot after the fact.) It involved—in the proudest tradition of Tony Soprano— whacking her opponent.

When Kerrigan was leaving the ice in Detroit after a practice session at the U.S. Figure Skating Championships, she was attacked by a man who clubbed her on her knee with a metal baton. While Kerrigan healed, Harding stepped in and won the U.S. title and a spot on the Olympic team, which would compete in Lillehammer the following month.

One of the conspirators, Shawn Eckhardt, told the FBI about the plot hatched by Gillooly as a way to clear the path for his wife to the Olympics by getting Kerrigan out of the way. Gillooly hired Shane Stant to hit Kerrigan on the knee.

The plot ultimately failed. Kerrigan, who had recovered from her injury, skated well in Lillehammer. Heading into the finals, she was in first place, just slightly ahead of Oksana Baiul and Surya Bonaly. Harding was tenth.

In the final long program skate, Baiul won a controversial slim 5–4 vote among the judges, beating Kerrigan, who won Olympic silver, by a slim margin. Harding finished well out of the medal competition.

In February 1994 Gillooly accepted a plea bargain in exchange for his testimony against Harding. Harding avoided further prosecution and any possible jail time by pleading guilty on March 16 of hindering the investigation of the attack and received three years' probation, five hundred hours of community service, and a fine of $160,000.

Shawn Eckhardt changed his name to Brian Sean Griffith after serving fourteen months of an eighteen-month prison term. He passed away in 2007 of natural causes at the age of forty.

At the end of June, the U.S. Figure Skating Association stripped Harding of her 1994 title and banned her for life from participating in any sanctioned events as either a skater or a coach. The organization's investigation concluded that Harding knew about the attack before it happened and displayed a disregard for fairness, good sportsmanship, and ethical behavior.

In ensuing years, Harding has been involved with several incidents that seem to have been influenced by alcohol. She also became a boxer before her career was cut short by asthma.

Kerrigan married her former agent, Jerry Solomon, and they have three children. She retired from active competition following the 1994 Olympics and has appeared in a variety of ice skating shows.

This supposedly serene sport was once again rocked by scandal at the Salt Lake City Olympics in 2002. This time, it was not the ladies' figure skating championship up for grabs, but the pairs' event, where Canadians Jamie Salé and David Pelletier were an attractive and talented pair poised to help Canada earn its third Olympic gold in figure skating; it had happened only twice before, in 1948 and 1960.

The pressure on the pair was intense but they had skated so proficiently to "Love Story" that it was obvious they had captured the gold. As they circled the ice following their stirring performance, the audience roared, "Six! Six!" in anticipation of a perfect score from the judges.

But when the scores were announced, Salé and Pelletier placed second; five judges had awarded the long program to Russian skaters Yelena Berezhnaya and Anton Sikharulidze, while the Canadian pair were scored highest by four judges.

The arena was silenced, and fans all over the world were shocked by questionable scores that gave the gold to the Russian pair. It was especially troubling since Sikharulidze did not land properly on one of his jumps, a double Axel.

The results infuriated all who had seen the competition and it didn't take long before questions of cheating came to the forefront. How was it possible that the Canadian pair didn't score well enough to capture gold? Quite frankly, because the fix was in.

Under a cloud of worldwide suspicion, French judge Marie-Reine Le Gougne quickly confessed that she had been pressured to vote for the Russian pair by the French skating federation. In exchange for the award of the long program to the Russian pair, the French ice dancing team of Marina Anissina and Gwendal Peizerat would get a first-place vote from the Russians.

The scandal resulted in the suspension of Le Gougne and French official Didier Gailhaguet and officials and Le Gougne's score was not counted, resulting in a tie. A second pair of gold medals was awarded to Salé and Pelletier in a special ceremony later in the week.

Months later, Italian authorities arrested a reputed Russian mobster Alimzahan Tokhtakthounov after the FBI accused him of being behind the fix. Any chance that he would face justice ended, however, when an Italian judge refused to allow his extradition to the United States.

The scandal also resulted in changes to the judging system. Anonymous judging was incorporated, with the rationale that it would free the judges from outside pressure regarding their vote. After two years of this system, the International Skating Union adopted an entirely new judging system, called the Code of Points, in 2003–2004.

Not all amateur cheating involves older athletes. One of the most unfortunate and best-remembered scandals involving amateur athletics includes Little League Baseball and a talented, overpowering left-handed pitcher named Danny Almonte.

The pitching phenom's Bronx, New York, team took third place in the 2001 Little League World Series. But right from the start, his mature appearance on the mound led to suspicions that this native of Moca, Dominican Republic, was older than the Little League maximum of twelve years of age. At one point, a team from Staten Island, New York, hired a private detective to look into the ages of Almonte and his teammates, as did a team from Pequannock Township, New Jersey. But the investigations failed to turn up any evidence that Almonte was not born on April 7, 1989, as his family insisted.

Inspired by the controversy, *Sports Illustrated* reporters Ian Thomsen and Luis Fernando Llosa began to delve into birth records in Moca after the end of the Little League classic. And in Moca, they found a notation that Felipe Almonte had registered his son's date of birth as April 7, 1987, at Dr. Torbio Bencosme Hospital.

On August 31 the Dominican national public records office announced that the hurler was actually born in 1987. The Little League declared him ineligible and forced his Baby Bombers team to forfeit all its tournament wins. Felipe Almonte and Rolando Paulino were banned from Little League for life, and Dominican prosecutors filed charges against the elder Almonte for falsifying a birth certificate.

For his part, Danny Almonte was not aware of the scam. He did not speak English at the time, and he just wanted to play baseball. Little League president Stephen Keener said that he and his teammates had been "used in a most contemptible and despicable way and that millions of Little Leaguers around the world were deceived."

In the fall of 2007, at the age of twenty, Danny Almonte enrolled as a freshman at Western Oklahoma State College in Altus, where he pitches and plays right field for the Pioneers.

Athletes often hone their skills in amateur competition before turning professional, where they can earn those sought-after big paydays. But there are many examples of how, in addition to refining their athletic abilities, they learn the benefits of cheating in the amateur ranks as well.

9

CREATING THE FRANKENSTEIN ATHLETE

The Drug Culture in Sports

"The use of performance-enhancing drugs like steroids in base-ball, football and other sports is dangerous, and it sends the wrong message—that there are shortcuts to accomplishment, and that performance is more important than character."

—President George W. Bush,
State of the Union address, January 20, 2004

As sure as the sports section in every morning newspaper across the country reviews sporting events from the previous day, an increasingly troublesome trend in the world of sports is that the morning paper also often includes news of yet another athlete's involvement in the use of illegal drugs. For many outside the sports spotlight, their only experiences with illegal drugs is the occasional use of the recreational kind. But in the high-powered world of sports, where fortune and fame can be decided by a millisecond, any means by which one athlete can gain even the slimmest edge has become acceptable. The drug culture in sports has reached such a crescendo that we've gone well beyond jocks doping to win events. Now, many are doping just trying to keep up with their competitors. It is a vicious circle that has fans doubting the validity of just about every outstanding athletic achievement.

If a big, powerful home run hitter like Ryan Howard hits a gargantuan tater, fans will whisper—even though most players are just like Ryan Howard: honest, hardworking, nondoping athletes who strive to be the best they can be the old-fashioned way. It's just not fair.

Most fans, who live their lives out of the spotlight and who have been so disappointed by so many athletes, are certainly against the use of performance-enhancing drugs—particularly when that use filters down to local college and high school athletes trying to ensure their piece of the pie. That's when it gets dangerous—and hits home.

The amateur and professional sports world has reacted—albeit a day late and a dollar short—in an attempt to put an end to the widespread use of illegal drugs on every level. But when confronted by talented, aggressive, extremely competitive athletes surrounded by throngs of enablers who also want *their* piece of the pie, the recipe for dishonest disaster is always percolating.

Unless our culture decides that it wants überleagues of doped-up, 'roided jocks with watermelon-sized heads and pea-sized testicles performing their sport as if there was no such thing as gravity, then stringent measures need to be taken.

We're only human, and many of us have opinions about issues we really don't understand. Just look at the wide variety of—sometimes underinformed—opinions about any political campaign or particularly controversial topic. So it seems prudent to take a step back and try to get a better understanding of just what we're dealing with.

Before talking about the use of steroids, particularly in baseball, history dictates that we should discuss greenies, otherwise known as peptos. Greenies are an amphetamine—speed—which helps a player boost his effort. But a clear distinction should be made between greenies and present-day steroids. Decades ago, players might pop a few greenies prior to a game or sip from a special pot of "hot" coffee in the clubhouse, which was for players only. Greenies helped players to get loose more quickly and play through stretches of the long season when they just weren't able to get up for the game. But greenies, unlike steroids and human growth hormone, did not enable a ballplayer to do things he was normally unable to do. Instead, they gave him what amounted to an extreme caffine rush to get in his ass in gear, loosen up, and play through pain or fatigue. But they never allowed anyone to play beyond his natural ability.

"You have to distinguish greenies, or peptos, as they were called, from steroids," says former pitcher Jim Bouton, who authored what might be the greatest book ever on baseball, *Ball Four*. "Greenies only allowed you to play up to your ability. If you didn't get a good night's sleep, or you had a hangover, it would allow you to play up to your ability, or at least some players thought that. It did not create a different human being. It did not change your physical makeup. It did not allow you to play beyond your ability, your normal ability, as steroids do and human growth hormone does.

"Greenies were performance *enablers*, not enhancers."

Greenies, named for the color of the pills, were introduced to the game in the 1940s. Amphetamines speed up the heart rate and have been proven to fight fatigue, increase alertness, and sharpen reaction time. They were actually considered harmless pep pills until 1970, when they were made illegal without a prescription. They have since been found to be addictive and can cause heart attacks and strokes.

Baseball's love affair with greenies officially ended before the start of the 2006 season, when Major League Baseball began testing players for them. Now, a player who fails the test once is sent to counseling. The second strike results in a twenty-five-game suspension.

The pharmaceutical industry—and baseball—have come a long way since the days of greenies, with the introduction of steroids. While everyone has an opinion about steroids, not as many people understand just what they are. What do steroids do to make the long-term health risks so acceptable to so many of today's athletes?

According to the National Institute on Drug Abuse, anabolic-androgenic steroids are man-made substances related to male sex hormones. "Anabolic" refers to muscle building and "androgenic" refers to increased masculine characteristics. "Steroids" is the name of the class of drug. These types of drugs are available legally only by prescription, to treat conditions that occur when the body produces abnormally low amounts of testosterone, such as in delayed puberty and some types of impotence. They can also be prescribed to treat body wasting in patients with AIDS and other diseases that result in loss of lean muscle mass. Abuse of anabolic steroids can lead to serious health issues, some of which are irreversible.

Today, athletes and others abuse anabolic steroids to enhance performance and improve physical appearance. Anabolic steroids can be taken orally or injected, and are used in cycles of weeks or months, rather than continuously, in a practice known as cycling. Users often combine several different types of steroids to maximize their effectiveness while minimizing negative effects. This is known as stacking.

The major side effects of anabolic steroid abuse include a litany of serious health issues, including liver tumors and cancer, jaundice (the yellowish color of skin, tissues, and body fluids), fluid retention, high blood pressure, and an increase in bad cholesterol and decrease in good cholesterol. Abusers may also suffer from kidney tumors, severe acne, and trembling.

Men who abuse steroids often suffer from gender-specific side effects such as shrinking of the testicles, reduced sperm count, infertility, baldness, development of breasts, and increased risk for prostate cancer. For women, side effects can include the growth of facial hair, male-pattern baldness, changes in or cessation of the menstrual cycle, enlargement of the clitoris, and a deepened voice.

And for adolescents who make the misguided decision to abuse steroids, side effects include permanently halted growth as a result of premature skeletal maturation and accelerated puberty changes. So adolescents risk being shorter than they would normally have been for the remainder of their lives.

"We have a guy in our book, Tim Montgomery, who said that if he could break the 100-meter record, he didn't care if he dropped dead after he crossed the finish line," says Lance Williams, coauthor of *Game of Shadows*. "In *Ball Four* by Jim Bouton, they have guys sitting in the bullpen talking about if you would take a pill that could make you become a twenty-game winner, even if it took five years off your life. Athletes are young men and women and they don't have the perspective that an older person—even in their thirties and forties—has. They think they'll never die. They think the future will never come. The rewards are so incredible. Financially, it's a tremendous temptation."

A 2005 report by the President's Council on Physical Fitness and Sports titled *Anabolic-Androgenic Steroids: Incidence of Use and Health Implications* treated the subject of steroid use and abuse in great detail. The report concludes: "Although anabolic steroids are illegal, and their use is banned by virtually every sport's governing body, survey and drug-testing data indicate continued use by competitive athletes at all levels. That fact that the level of steroid use appears to have increased significantly over the past three decades among adolescents, women, and recreational athletes is also of growing concern. The use of anabolic steroids presents an interesting public health challenge. While these drugs are associated with deleterious physical and psychological outcomes, they are being used to achieve what many consider socially desirable ends: being physically attractive and being a winner."

But, as so many sports fans have learned over the past decade, steroids are not the only synthetic drugs of choice by today's injectors. Human growth hormone is another well-known performance-enhancing drug that many don't understand. The difference between steroids and HGH can be described as follows: steroids are like heroin while HGH is like marijuana. Unlike steroids, HGH has not been proven to increase weight-lifting ability and it has a greater effect on muscle definition than it does on muscle strength.

So why would an athlete risk suspension and suspicion by using HGH? On the surface, it makes no sense. A baseball player can beef up on steroids and improve his performance as a result. HGH, on the other hand, is often used to attempt to reverse the effects of aging. What's the connection?

"One possibility is that the drug really does enhance performance but that the effect is too subtle to measure in a controlled setting," according to Daniel Engber in "The Growth Hormone Myth: What Athletes, Fans and the Sports Media Don't Understand about HGH," at *Slate*. "An elite athlete might be able to detect very slight improvements in strength and agility that would be invisible to lab scientists or statistical tests. At the highest levels of sport, a tiny edge can make a big difference. Athletes might also derive some added benefit by mixing HGH with other drugs—anti-aging doctors often prescribe growth hormone in combination with testosterone.

"It's also possible that baseball players aren't using HGH to beef up at all. Almost everyone who gets caught red-handed claims they were using the drug to recover from an injury. This might be more than a ploy to win sympathy: Some doctors believe that growth hormone can speed up tissue repair. There isn't much clinical work to support this idea, however.

"The most likely reason that athletes use HGH, though, is superstition. A ballplayer might shoot up with HGH for the same reason we take vitamin C when we have a cold: There's no good reason to think it does anything, but we're willing to give it a try. The fact that the major sports leagues have banned growth hormone only encourages the idea that the drug has tangible benefits. Why would they ban something unless it worked?

"This mentality has put doping officials and athletes into a feedback loop of added hysteria. The World Anti-Doping Agency (WADA) will ban any drug that athletes use, whether or not it has an effect. The WADA code points out that the use of substances, 'based on the mistaken belief they enhance performance is clearly contradictory to the spirit of sport.' In other words, it doesn't matter if HGH gives athletes an unfair advantage. If Jerry Hairston believes he's cheating, then he really is cheating."

According to the Mitchell Report, which investigated and reported on the use of illegal steroids and human growth hormone in professional baseball, it seems that many of the players implicated for the use of HGH were actually trying to recover from an injury. Whether the drug actually does speed up tissue repair, thus enabling players to recover and return sooner from injury, is not known for certain. What is known is that growth hormone stimulates the synthesis of collagen, which is necessary for strengthening cartilage, bones, tendons, and ligaments.

Jason Grimsley reportedly used the drug in combination with the anabolic steroid Deca-Durabolin to recover from ligament replacement in just nine months—half the usual estimated recovery time for pitchers.

When you combine anabolic steroids and HGH, the result is apparently very conducive and potent—sort of like combining a triple espresso martini with a double shot of Jägermeister. The stronger connective tissues developed through the use of HGH not only work better and heal faster, but they are better equipped to handle the oversized muscles often associated with steroid use.

HGH also increases red blood cell count, boosts heart function, and makes more energy available by stimulating the breakdown of fat. Users also have noticed improved eyesight, better sleep, and better sex.

HGH users can sometimes be identified by the characteristic side effects of the hormone. Use of HGH can cause acromegaly, a condition characterized by excessive growth of the head, feet, and hands. In people with acromegaly, the lips, nose, tongue, jaw, and forehead increase in size, and fingers and toes can widen. Excessive use of HGH can also lead to diabetes.

Another drug that has made the rounds among athletes is andro, short for androstenedione, which was manufactured as a dietary supplement. Andro—a hormone produced in the adrenal glands that increases testosterone production and protein synthesis, resulting in increased lean body mass and strength during training—was commonly used by MLB players, including Mark McGwire, throughout the 1990s.

On March 12, 2004, the Anabolic Steroid Control Act of 2004 was introduced into the United States Senate. It amended the Controlled Substances Act of 1970, placing both anabolic steroids and prohormones on a list of controlled substances and making possession of the banned substances a federal crime. The law took effect on January 20, 2005.

When McGwire was attacking record home run seasons, he openly admitted to taking andro, which was, at the time, a legal over-the-counter muscle enhancement product. So when he took andro, McGwire was not breaking any rules—either those of baseball or those of society.

But the abuse of such dangerous substances by athletes did not just begin with steroids and other performance-enhancing drugs. They are simply the latest of an ever-growing list of dangerous man-made substances used to help create the Frankenstein Athlete. The history goes well beyond even the historical period where Mary Shelley wrote *Frankenstein* in 1831.

We've seen the impact of pharmaceuticals on performance on the field, but it will be interesting and perhaps tragic to see what health-related ramifications drug use will have on these athletes later in life. They may have raised the bar significantly on the playing field. What happens in their future is a crapshoot, because this past generation of performance-enhanced athletes are also guinea pigs who may very well pay a huge price for their athletic achievements.

Has our society become aware of the problem soon enough? Will the risks of such behavior preclude future jocks from crossing over the line? The United States has yet to experience the long-term effect of the use of steroids and performance-enhancing substances, but the same cannot be said of other countries.

10

SON OF FRANKENSTEIN

The Tradition of Doping: A Sad Sports Legacy

"My trainer told me the pills were vitamins, but I soon had cramps in my legs, my voice became gruff and sometimes I couldn't talk any more. Then I started to grow a moustache and my periods stopped."

—East German sprinter Renate Neufeld

It is literally impossible to find the first case of doping in athletics. As described in chapter 8, ancient Greek athletes used to prep for the early Olympic Games by drinking special potions made with wine, in hopes of gaining some winning advantage. They also ate large quantities of meat, as well as animal hearts and testicles, to perform better. Drug use and abuse was a serious issue in sports long before the Mitchell Report.

The precursor to bicycling endurance races were walking races held early in the nineteenth century. In 1807 Abraham Wood admitted that he used opium to keep himself awake for twenty-four hours against Robert Barclay Allardyce. By 1877, walking races had extended to five hundred miles, drawing twenty thousand spectators to watch the event every day. Promoters then got the idea to have the same courses run with cyclists, who were, at the time, the fastest humans on earth.

The popularity of these six-day cycle races spread from Germany and England across the Atlantic Ocean to the United States, where they also became a great spectator event once they started to be held at Madison Square Garden in New York in 1891. More and more people paid more and more money to see the event, which prompted the participants to be more and more inventive when trying to find ways to stay awake and alert longer than their competitors. As it had throughout the history of sports, the almighty dollar won out at all costs.

The riders had trainers who assisted them during the events. One of the treatments they provided included nitroglycerine, a drug often used by heart patients. It stimulates the heart, which helped improve the breathing of the riders. And trainers often supplied riders with treatments made with a base of cocaine in order to help them find their "second wind" during the six-day events. But many riders suffered from hallucinations as a result of exhaustion—and, very possibly, the use of the drugs. At one point, American champion Major Taylor dropped out of the New York race. "I cannot go on with safety," he said. "For there is a man chasing me around the ring with a knife in his hand."

We have already discussed the skullduggery of marathon runner Fred Lorz in the 1904 Olympics. But the man who was awarded the gold medal, Thomas Hicks, had some unnatural assistance from his trainer Charles Lucas, who injected the runner with a hypodermic needle as he began to founder.

"I therefore decided to inject him with a milligram of sulphate of strychnine and to make him drink a large glass brimming with brandy," Lucas said after the race. "He set off again as best he could but he needed another injection four miles from the end to give him a semblance of speed and to get him to the finish." Not exactly a shot of V-8.

In the early years of the twentieth century, strychnine was seen as a useful aid to runners in long-distance races. It should be noted that Hicks spent time between life and death, but eventually recovered to be awarded his gold medal. But he never raced again.

Cycling—especially long-distance cycling—is a demanding sport, so it is only natural that the Tour de France would see its fair share of attempts at dishonesty. As early as 1924, involvement of some of the racers with drugs was publicly known.

Henri Pelissier, the winner of the 1923 Tour de France, showed a reporter for the French newspaper *Le Petit Parisien* what kind of help he was given to race well.

"You have no idea what the Tour de France is," he said. "It's a Calvary. Worse than that, because the road to the Cross has only 14 stations and ours has 15. We suffer from the start to the end. You want to know how we keep going?" At that point he pulled out a vial from his bag. "That's cocaine, for our eyes. This is chloroform, for our gums. At night in our rooms, we can't sleep. We twitch and dance the jig about as though we were doing St. Vitus's Dance. There's less flesh on our bodies than on a skeleton."

He also said the racers were white as shrouds once the dirt of the racing day was cleaned off: in addition to these other challenges, their bodies were drained by diarrhea. The spoils of victory seem a long way off when considering what these athletes endured to win.

In 1930 the race changed to national teams that were paid for by the organizers. But the rule book that was distributed to the riders reminded them that drugs were not among the items with which they would be provided.

While the introduction of steroids and other performance-enhancing substances is a relatively new element in the sports world, we have previously learned of the tradition of baseball players and other athletes using amphetamines. This was not something that just happened in the 1960s and 1970s. One amphetamine, Benzedrine, was produced as early as 1887 and was isolated in the United States in 1934. British troops reportedly used 72 million amphetamine tablets during World War II, and according to one report, the Royal Air Force went through so many pills that it was said that methedrine won the Battle of Britain.

But the dangers of such drugs quickly became apparent. Danish rider Knud Enemark Jensen collapsed and later died during a time trial at the 1960 Olympic Games in Rome. An autopsy discovered that he had taken amphetamines and Ronical, a drug that dilates the blood vessels.

While athletes boosted their energy levels with the use of amphetamines and other drugs, chemists and doctors were experimenting with testosterone, which seemed to help those who took it to gain more weight and strength than any regular training regime. The anabolic steroid methandrostenolone was first made in the United States in 1958 by the pharmaceutical company Ciba. As time evolved, the evolution of steroids and steroid use continued.

The East German Olympic team had become a major player in the sporting world in the 1970s and 1980s. A relatively small country boasting less than 17 million people, the East Germans began to overmatch other countries—including the United States and Russia—in international sporting contests. In just four years, the number of gold medals won by East Germany doubled from twenty to forty.

After the end of the Cold War, with the dismantling of the Iron Curtain, some troubling realizations came to the forefront of the sports world. Word came out that trainers and coaches had used steroids and other performance-enhancing drugs to ensure athletic superiority, giving East Germany an unfair advantage while putting the health of their own young charges at great risk. The athletes themselves were told the substances they were being given were vitamins.

The special pills combined with a demanding training schedule to make East Germany a force to be reckoned with in amateur athletics. In subsequent years, many of those athletes reported serious medical consequences, from liver cancer, organ damage, psychological defects, hormonal changes, and infertility. It was only after the fall of the Berlin Wall in 1989 that East German athletes came forward to explain the frequent doses of "vitamins" and needles they had been given.

Three of the athletes who came forward had been members of the East German swimming team. Kornelia Ender won four gold and four silver medals at the 1972 and 1976 Olympic Games. She said she had been given injections since the age of thirteen. Barbara Krause, a three-time Olympic gold medalist and an eight-time world record holder, was forced out of the 1976 games because team doctors miscalculated the doses of the drugs they gave her and feared that she might test positive at the games. And Carola Nitschke was also just thirteen when doctors began to inject her with steroids and the male hormone testosterone.

One of East Germany's premier sprinters, Renate Neufeld, fled to the West and told her tale of drug use—drugs supplied to her by her coaches as she trained to represent her country in the 1980 Olympics.

"At 17, I joined the East Berlin Sports Institute," she told *Sport Informations Dienst* in December 1978. "My specialty was the 80m hurdles. We swore that we would never speak to anyone about our training methods, including our parents. The training was very hard. We were all watched. We signed a register each time we left for dormitory and we had to say where we were going and what time we would return. One day, my trainer, Gunter Clam, advised me to take pills to improve my performance. I was running 200m in 24 seconds. My trainer told me the pills were vitamins, but I soon had cramp in my legs, my voice became gruff and sometimes I couldn't talk any more. Then I started to grow a moustache and my periods stopped. I then refused to take these pills. One morning in October 1977, the secret police took me at 7 a.m. and questioned me about my refusal to take pills prescribed by the trainer. I then decided to flee with my fiancé."

When she came to the West, she brought with her grey tablets and a green powder that she said had been given to her and other members of her club by doctors and officials. They were identified as anabolic steroids.

The German government brought many of the doctors and coaches to trial. In one such trial, the former East German sports official Manfred Ewals and his medical director, Manfred Hoeppner, were found responsible for what the German court called the "systematic and overall doping in competitive sports." But Ewals received only a twenty-two-month suspended sentence. Two doctors from the Sport Club Dynamo, which was a well-known doping center, were brought to trial. Dieter Binus and Bernd Pansold were both found guilty of administering hormones to underage female athletes from 1975 to 1984.

Much of the time, athletes were drugged without their knowledge. It is estimated that nearly ten thousand former athletes have suffered the physical and emotional effects of drug abuse. A special Internet site was created by doping victims trying to gain justice and compensation.

While these athletes will have to deal with the health effects resulting from the unconscionable behavior of their sports officials who gave them drugs without their knowledge, there are a plethora of athletes from all sports and many countries who doped knowingly. In the eyes of many of these already world-class athletes, the benefits far outweigh any consequences.

It took Canadian sprinter Ben Johnson just 9.79 seconds to capture the 100m gold medal at the Seoul Olympics in 1988. But it could be argued that it took even less time for him to lose the affection of an entire country when it was discovered that he had flunked a drug test. At the conclusion of the race, in which Johnson beat his primary competitor, Carl Lewis, he noted that he would have been even faster had he not raised his hand in the air just before crossing the finish line.

Sadly, his urine samples were found to contain Stanozolol, and he was disqualified three days later. He eventually admitted having used steroids when he set his 1987 world record, and that record was later rescinded.

Johnson and many other athletes caught cheating in this manner argued that they were doping to keep up with the other top runners who were using drugs on a regular basis—that they were simply trying to make it a more even playing field. Those complaints might be based in reality in light of information that has since been made public that four of the top five finishers in the 100-meter race at the 1988 Olympics all tested positive for banned substances at some point in their careers.

Regardless, Johnson was banned from competing for two years and stripped of all the other world titles and records he held, in addition to his Olympic gold medal. He began racing again in 1991, but was never able to reach the same heights as when he was considered the fastest man in the world.

In 1993 he once again tested positive for steroids at a meet in Montreal. By unanimous decision, the International Association of Athletics Federations banned him from competition for life.

Marion Jones was the darling of the Sydney Olympic Games of 2000 after winning five medals—including three gold—for the United States. She was beautiful, feminine, and charming on camera. She sprinted into the record books as the first woman to win five medals in a single Olympics. She became a cover girl, featured on the cover of *Vogue*, and companies were lining up to make her the center of their advertising campaigns.

A basketball star at the University of North Carolina, Jones changed her focus strictly to track in time for the 1997 World Championships in Athens. In 1998, she met and married shot-putter C. J. Hunter, who introduced her to Trevor Graham, a new coach who helped her make technical changes that prepared her for the Sydney Games in 2000.

But as Jones was winning gold, it was revealed that Hunter (who had withdrawn from the games due to a knee injury) had tested pos-

Marion Jones appears during a press conference. Associated Press/Don Ryan.

itive four times over the summer for the banned steroid nandrolone. Their marriage soon ended, but Jones continued her working relationship with Graham and began working with Victor Conte, the nutritionist who founded BALCO. She began a relationship with sprinter Tim Montgomery, with whom she had a son. But news of Montgomery's doping soon became known, and he was striped of his awards and records in December 2005. As was the case with Hunter, these new stories cast more suspicion on Jones, who vehemently denied using any banned substances.

But by then she was using drugs supplied by Conte, and Graham (who had become Conte's adversary as a result of their competition for the same group of athletic clients) sent the syringe laced with steroids to the USADA. The resulting raid on the BALCO headquarters netted authorities evidence that Jones had in fact used steroids, her denials notwithstanding.

Conte appeared on the national television news program *20/20* and stated that he had seen Jones inject herself with HGH and that he had supplied her with five different performance-enhancing drugs prior to, during, and after the 2000 Olympics. As a result, the International Olympic Committee immediately began an investigation of Jones based on the allegations by Conte, whom she sued for defamation.

Still attempting to regain her form on the track, Jones failed a drug test in August 2006. She married fellow sprinter Obadele Thompson in February 2007, and they had a child in July. But that October, she finally pleaded guilty to lying about her steroid use to U.S. investigators and admitted that she had taken steroids before the Sydney Games, where she captured the hearts of so many fans.

She was stripped of her titles and sentenced to six months in prison. After admitting her guilt, she said, "I want to apologize to all of you for this. I am very sorry for disappointing you all in so many ways."

In July 2008 the U.S. Anti-Doping Agency gave Trevor Graham a lifetime ban for his role in helping athletes obtain performance-enhancing drugs. Graham was banned from participating in any event sanctioned by the U.S. Olympic Committee, the IAAF, USA Track and Field, or any other group that participates in the World Anti-Doping Agency program.

He was convicted in May 2008 of lying to federal investigators about his relationship to an admitted steroid dealer, but has not yet been sentenced. Graham was previously banned from all USOC-sponsored facilities.

Doping questions and scandals continue to plague the Tour de France. Two of the best-known names in the sports world are Lance Armstrong and Floyd Landis, both winners of the Tour de France. Armstrong has rebounded from questions about his own possible drug use, while Landis has been vehement in denying illegal drug use during the race but has still failed to clear his name. While Armstrong and Landis have been two of the more controversial figures to participate in the tournament, they are far from the first cyclists to make headlines.

The Tour de France began in 1903. It is a twenty-three-day event consisting of twenty-one stages that is usually run over more than twenty-two hundred miles. The race is broken into stages from one town to another, each of which is an individual race. The time taken to complete each stage is added up, and a cumulative time for each rider decides the winner at the conclusion of the tournament.

Competitors enter the race as part of a team, and there are normally more than twenty teams with nine riders each. Each team is known by the name of its sponsor and wears a distinctive jersey. Riders assist their teammates and have access to a team car, which is similar to a pit crew that moves.

The race itself alternates between clockwise and counterclockwise tours of France. A feature of the race has always been the mountains. Mountain passes like the Toumalet in the Pyrenees have been made famous by the race. The steepness of the climb is a testament to the physical ability of the riders. Competing at this level requires a combination of endurance and strength. In fact, a 2006 article in the *New York Times* noted, "The Tour de France is arguably the most physiologically demanding of athletic events, like running a marathon several days a week for nearly three weeks."

While they are extremely competitive during the stages of the race, the riders also must observe an unwritten code of conduct. For instance, whenever possible, a rider is allowed to lead the race through his hometown or on his birthday. It is considered unsporting to attack a leading rider who is delayed by a mechanical problem, who is taking a food break, or who needs to use the restroom.

That said, it remains a sport driven by money and fame—a dangerous combination when competitive athletes are put in the mix. And allegations of doping have been part of the race since its inception. In 1967 Tom Simpson, a British cyclist, died while climbing Mont Vertoux after he used amphetamines, whose harmful effects were exacerbated by the fact that racers of that era generally drank very little water.

The 1998 race was called the Tour of Shame when the entire Festina team was excluded after it was discovered that the team car contained large amounts of various performance-enhancing drugs. The team director later admitted that some of the cyclists were routinely given banned substances. Six other teams pulled out in protest, including the Dutch TVM team, who left the Tour still being questioned by the police. The ultimate winner of the 1998 Tour was Marco Pantani, but he later failed a drug test as well.

As a result, race organizers and the International Cycling Union (UCI) introduced more antidoping measures in the years that followed, including more frequent testing of riders and new tests for blood doping. And the independent World Anti-Doping Agency was formed in 1999.

The increased testing procedures were an important element in the Lance Armstrong controversy. The seven-time Tour champion, an American hero for his valiant battle against cancer, has been accused of doping in published reports. In August 2005, shortly after his seventh consecutive victory, the French newspaper *l'Equipe* claimed that it found evidence that Armstrong had used erythropoietin, which can be used as a blood doping agent, in the 1999 Tour de France. He denied the allegations, and an investigation by the International Cycling Union later reported that Armstrong had not engaged in doping.

At that same race, Armstrong's urine had traces of glucocorticosteroid hormones, although the amount detected was well below the legal limit. He explained that he had used the skin cream Cemalyt, which contains triamcinolone, to treat saddle sores. Armstrong had previously received permission from the International Cycling Union to use the cream.

Floyd Landis has not been as fortunate as Armstrong. Landis was the winner of the 2006 Tour de France. His thrilling win eased cycling fans' pain at seeing two top riders, Jan Ulrich and Ivan Basso, banned by their teams earlier in the race for doping allegations—but the relief was only temporary.

About to enter stage 17 of the event, Landis was far behind the leaders, rated a 70–1 shot to win. But he won that stage by an astounding six minutes, leaving him just thirty seconds behind the leader. He pulled to the lead and eventually won the Tour de France by fifty-seven seconds.

But four days after his apparent victory, Landis had a positive test for testosterone imbalance in his initial test sample following his stage 17 victory. His second sample also detected an imbalance. He was fired from the Phonak Hearing Systems team on August 5, after a test result indicated an abnormally high testosterone/epitestosterone ratio. He was stripped of his title and given a two-year suspension from professional racing. All of his appeals have subsequently been denied.

Landis continues his thus-far-unsuccessful attempt to clear his name and regain his championship. In May 2007, an arbitration hearing began between the USADA and Landis regarding the doping allegations. On September 20, 2007, the arbitrators found Landis guilty of doping.

After Landis forfeited his Tour title, the second-place rider, Oscar Pereiro , became the race's official winner. The decision of whether to strip Landis of his title was made by the International Cycling Union. Under UCI rules, the determination of whether or not a cyclist violated any rules must be made by the cyclist's national federation—in this case USA Cycling, which transferred the case to the USADA.

Landis agreed not to participate in any racing in France in 2007, which allowed him to postpone a hearing of his case there for as long as possible while he continued to ride in other countries. On December 19, 2007, the French Anti-Doping Agency found him guilty of doping and issued a two-year suspension, barring him from racing in France until early 2009.

In July 2008 Landis's final appeal was denied by the Court of Arbitration for Sport. He will not regain the title he won with the stunning comeback in stage 17, a rally many thought was just too good to be true—and that turned out to be aided by synthetic testosterone.

The CAS also indicated that Landis must pay $100,000 toward the legal fees incurred by the USADA in bringing the case.

In response to revelations about doping, many countries have created their own antidoping authorities. The USADA is the official independent antidoping agency for Olympic-related sports in the United States. It was created on October 1, 2000, as a result of recommendations made by the United States Olympic Committee's Select Task Force on Externalization to uphold the Olympic ideal of fair play and to represent the interests of Olympic, Pan-American Games, and Paralympic athletes.

The USADA began operations on October 1, 2000, and was given full authority to execute a comprehensive national antidoping program encompassing testing, adjudication, education, and research and to develop programs, policies, and procedures in each of those areas.

"USADA believes that deterring the use of drugs in sport is necessary to preserve the integrity of sport in the United States," says USADA CEO Terry Madden. "Athletes, including children who dream of athletic success, have a fundamental right to believe that they do not need to use drugs to compete. USADA is dedicated to protecting that right and welcomes the opportunity to work with any sport that is committed to the cause of drug-free sport."

The organization focuses on four primary areas: research, education, testing, and results management. Research is the cornerstone of the program, with $2 million allocated annually toward the study of prohibited substances, the development of tests and other issues involved with the practice of doping in sport. Education focuses on the ethics involved with the use of performance-enhancing substances and the associated health risks. Testing is done on both in- and out-of-competition athletes. Results management and the adjudication process were designed to eliminate the conflicts of interest inherent with the involvement of national governing bodies in prosecuting and sanctioning their own athletes.

"While the USADA continues to concentrate on the basic areas of testing, results management, research, and education, it recognizes that real progress can only be achieved through effective interaction with athletes, national governing bodies, international federations, other national antidoping agencies and WADA," says Madden.

11

VICTOR CONTE

The Pied Piper of BALCO

"Victor was certainly the mastermind of the biggest doping scandal in history."

—Lance Williams, coauthor of *Game of Shadows*

"Many of these athletes were already using drugs, buying them out of the trunk of a car, not being tested or monitored. I brought it into a clinical laboratory and showed them their testing and they realized it was safe and effective."

—Victor Conte

Victor Conte, founder of the Bay Area Laboratory Co-operative (BALCO), has never been one to shy away from publicity. He is a leader and a promoter, of himself and others. But in fairness, this famous and, in some eyes, infamous mastermind of what may have been the biggest single scandal in the history of sports, is honest to a fault. He never hesitates to speak, and when he speaks, he does so honestly. The proof is in the pudding; as of this writing, all the accusations and revelations he has made have been proven true—each and every one—regardless of the denials, press conferences, and lawsuits that have had a way of just fading to black. To put it bluntly, when it comes to Victor Conte in the post-BALCO era, there is no such thing as bullshit.

The former bassist in the 1970s band Tower of Power, Conte founded BALCO in 1984 under the name of Millbrae Holistic, a San Francisco vitamin shop. The following year, Conte opened BALCO, a sports supplement company. One of the many things that set Conte apart from his competition was his investment in an ICP spectrometer, which he used to test athletes' blood and urine for mineral deficiencies; he used this information to produce and maintain the perfect balance of minerals in the body. In 1988 he offered free blood and urine tests to a group of athletes known as the BALCO Olympians. As a result, he was allowed to attend that year's Summer Olympics in Seoul, South Korea.

Conte was not involved with any illegal substances for years. He was a self-made and educated nutritionist who tried to help athletes honestly. He liked them and cared about them personally. But as his involvement in big-time athletics grew, he also saw rampant, widespread steroid use. At some point his mind-set became: If you can't beat 'em, join 'em. But when he ultimately did it, Conte blew away his competition.

"I have been working with Olympic athletes in 1984," says Conte, author of the book *BALCO: The Straight Dope on Steroids, Barry Bonds, Marion Jones and What We Can Do to Save Sports.* "I had worked with twenty-five in 1988 and they brought back fifteen medals at Seoul, which was about 20 percent of the U.S. winners. When I got back an Olympic official told me there were more positive drug tests in Seoul than just Ben Johnson. He told me that there were three U.S. athletes, two of which were the biggest names, who also tested positive and it was covered up. This continued through 1992, when Gregg Tafralis, a discus thrower had tested positive at the U.S. trials. I called Gregg and he was very upset, thinking he'd be banned. A few days later I got a call from an official who told me that my boy was off the hook. It seems that the testers weren't really trying to catch anybody.

"I began to realize that there was a culture that has existed for five decades that the use of performance enhancing drugs is rampant and has been. Those who have the money and capacity to create effective antidoping policies and procedures don't want to and they cover them up. All of a sudden, in 1999 I met Patrick Arnold and he told me he had some stuff [another word for illegal performance-enhancing drug] I might want to try that may not be detectable [in drug screenings]. I was able to send in some samples to a lab on a blind basis and they tested totally clean. Here was something that would not create a positive test. It turned out to be "the Clear." Arnold had copied it right out of the Merck index.

"Nobody was testing positive, so I did a lot of testing to determine the appropriate frequency of usage. At that point I made the decision to go down the slippery slope as opposed to being a bystander. My rationale was that I could help these athletes to do what they were already doing, but in a safe and effective manner. I tested them routinely for liver and kidney function at my lab."

One of the questions Conte often encounters is about a seeming inconsistency: He genuinely cared about his BALCO athletes, yet he supplied them with performance-enhancing drugs that have been proved hazardous to their health. To the contrary, Conte feels he actually made the use of these drugs safer for his athletes.

"There is a big difference between drinking a glass of red wine with a meal a couple times a week as opposed to drinking a gallon a day," he says. "Used responsibly, tests show that testosterone does not cause serious health issues. The *New England Journal of Medicine* in 1996 wrote that subjects who took 600 mg as opposed to the regular dosage of 200 mg had little effect except that a small percentage had developed slight acne and nothing else. I have worked with athletes who were taking 5,000 mg per week as opposed to 200 mg. Anabolic steroids, when abused, do cause adverse health effects. We're talking about degree. Taken in low doses, they can make you feel the best you've ever felt in your life, they'll make you stronger and give increased energy. I've used them and not abused them.

"I'm not recommending that athletes or anyone else should use super levels of performance-enhancing drugs, because they will cause problems with your health. I gave athletes drugs in three-week-on, one-week-off intervals. They had a total of ten days off a month. If they didn't do it that way, they didn't get more drugs.

"Many of these athletes were already using drugs, buying them out of the trunk of a car, not being tested or monitored. I brought it into a clinical laboratory and showed them their testing and they realized it was safe and effective."

Initially Conte treated mineral shortages in athletes, elevating their level of physical wellness. In 1996 he began working with football star Bill Romanowski, which opened the doors for other high-profile clients. A partnership he formed with former sprint coach Remi Korchemny resulted in the foundation of what they called the ZMA Track Club, which included such superstars as Marion Jones and Tim Montgomery.

Arnold, an organic chemist, was known from his development of androstenedione (andro), which came into prominence in 1996, when St. Louis Cardinals slugger Mark McGwire openly displayed it in his locker.

It was Arnold who created the designer steroid tetrahydrogestrinone, which is also known as THG or "the Clear." Along with two other anabolic steroids, norbolethone and desoxymethyltestosterone (DMT), these new, hard-to-detect steroids revolutionized the darker side of sports and helped bring BALCO and Conte into the limelight. Other designer steroids created by Arnold included human growth hormone, modafinil, testosterone cream, and erythropoietin, a hormone naturally produced by the body that improves the ability of red blood cells to transport oxygen.

This is a particularly important discovery, because when artificially introduced into the body, EPO allows red blood cells to carry greater amounts of oxygen, enabling the muscles to work longer and recover more quickly than usual. HGH is a hormone used to treat children diagnosed as pituitary dwarves. In theory, it builds muscle mass, increases height, helps with calcium retention in the body, reduces fat, helps with the immune system, and can reverse the aging process.

Testosterone cream—known as "the Cream"—is a salve that, when rubbed on the body, introduces testosterone, helping to trim body fat and build muscle. Even though it is less effective than testosterone shots, "the Cream" was widely used because it didn't cause a significant rise in the normal testosterone levels that are examined in drug tests.

Tetrahydrogestrinone, or "the Clear," is a designer anabolic steroid that affects users in much the same fashion as other anabolic steroids, making them bigger and stronger. But unlike most anabolic steroids, "the Clear" was not detectable on drug tests. THG was the main steroid used by BALCO. As Conte's athletes continued to be successful in their sports, more and more athletes came on board with him, taking THG and other new drugs manufactured by Arnold and distributed by personal trainer Greg Anderson.

"He was a guy who clearly wanted to be in the middle of things," says Mark Fainaru-Wada, coauthor of *Game of Shadows*, of Conte. "He's a high-energy, attention-getting kind of guy who could always make things happen. Victor always needed to be in the limelight. Around the mid- to late 1990s, he started providing performance-enhancing drugs to Bill Romanowski. He was the first guy, but then Victor provided performance-enhancing drugs to a wide variety of athletes in other sports as well."

Word spread quickly and other athletes from literally every sport followed, making Victor Conte look like the Pied Piper to gold medals and new records. He was one of the most popular people in the sports world, rubbing elbows with the best of the best.

"Victor was certainly the mastermind of the biggest doping scandal in history," says author Lance Williams. "And he was the mastermind, or master marketer, of it. As his attorney said, thank goodness that Victor has a narcissistic personality disorder. If he kept his mouth shut and kept a low and discreet profile, this could have gone on for years. But he couldn't keep his mouth shut about what he was doing with people.

"And it's no wonder why. Look at the Olympics. He had the world record holder in the hundred-meter, Marion Jones, won five gold medals and was the darling of the Olympics; he has other guys with Super Bowl rings; the greatest home run hitter of all time. It's hard to argue that he didn't have a significant effect on modern sports.

"He became a nutritionist who wanted to rub elbows with elite athletes and become important. Obviously, nutrition has such a limited impact on performance as opposed to banned drugs. He just wanted to be a player, and being a provider of sophisticated banned drugs was the way to do it.

"But I don't think he set out to be a steroid dealer. The rest of us just didn't realize, and I'm sure that he didn't realize that even back in the 1980s that track and field was infused with steroids. Nobody realized it at the time."

Just a partial list of BALCO clients resembles a Who's Who in Athletic Excellence. In addition to baseball's home run king Bonds and track star Jones, Conte also had in his stable the world's fastest human, Tim Montgomery; football players like Romanowski, All-Pro linebacker Bryce Paup, running backs Terrell Davis and Terry Kirby, and All-Pro defensive end Neil Smith; and other athletes, including

Zhanna Block, Regina Jacobs, Kevin Toth, Dwain Chambers, Kelli White, Michelle Collins, Corinne Shigemoto, Mac Wilkins, and a vast number of bodybuilders.

BALCO continued to grow and garner attention in the athletic community. But in 2002, a federal investigation of the company began amid allegations that world-class professional athletes were illegally receiving anabolic steroids and other performance-enhancing drugs from BALCO. Athletes were also reportedly having their steroid intake monitored there.

At the same time the federal investigation got underway, the USADA also began an investigation of BALCO. The biggest break in the case came the following fall, when the USADA received a syringe that was traced to BALCO containing small amounts of THG. As it turned out, the person who tipped off the USADA by sending them the syringe was Trevor Graham, a coach of both Marion Jones and Tim Montgomery. Not only did the tip break the investigation wide open, but using the sample of THG present in the syringe, drug testers were able to finally screen for the once untraceable drug at sporting events.

"Trevor Graham acted out of jealousy and greed," Conte says. "Trevor Graham did not like me. He was coaching people and then I agreed to help Tim Montgomery, who felt that Trevor was just not the right coach to help him. I assembled a whole team and recruited Charlie Francis, who was there because he had been banned. Trevor didn't like that. They had a nickname for Trevor, Stop Watch, because that's all he did. Charlie wrote all the programs. I had the power and Trevor resented me.

Trevor Graham exits the Federal Building in San Francisco. Associated Press/Ben Margot.

"I made the decision to terminate Trevor, who was doing all sorts of bad things. His deal was to give drugs to female athletes in exchange for sex. He'd say if you want to run like Marion Jones, wave this baton. I gave him some stuff for himself that he would up selling to other athletes. He could not be trusted.

"We were direct competitors, and I was beating Trevor regularly. He had some of the remaining Clear and sent it in anonymously in June 2002. In September of 2002 Trevor sent in the second sample, the syringe, and named me and all the BALCO athletes. This time they had more materials and they had the names."

There was plenty of irony surrounding Graham's selling out of Victor Conte, because BALCO's founder was doing the same thing to Graham. There was obviously great distrust and animosity brewing between the two.

"Trevor Graham says he was trying to clean up sport," says Williams. "Victor says he was trying to take out the competition. Track and field is a place where everybody knows everybody else. Trevor had worked a little bit with Victor and then they broke. When the Feds were going through the dumpster at BALCO, they found a letter that Victor wrote to the Olympic doping authorities alleging that Trevor was doping Victor's athletes. Trevor was dropping a dime on somebody he didn't like."

While some of the key players in this scandal, including Jones and Bonds, have been charged with perjury, Graham has not. He faced three counts of violating Title 18 of the United States Code (Section 1001), which prohibits the act of knowingly and willfully lying to government officials concerning any matter that is within the jurisdiction of the federal government. Graham was not being charged with lying under oath to a grand jury. Rather, he was believed to have knowingly lied to government officials while they were investigating BALCO.

After becoming a snitch against BALCO, how and why did Graham fall from the good graces of the investigators?

"The case against Graham rests on his statements to investigators, who originally found Graham to be a willing and knowledgeable source of BALCO information," wrote Michael McCann in a May 2008 *Sports Illustrated* article titled, "Graham Trial Could Expose Previously Untainted Athletes." "Graham had a rivalry of sorts with BALCO's president and founder Victor Conte, whom Graham believed was giving certain sprinters an unfair advantage by supplying them with steroids. Conte thought the same of Graham and the sprinters he coached. Graham, however, upped the ante by anonymously mailing to the U.S. Anti-Doping Agency a syringe that would ultimately prove that Conte was dealing steroids. The syringe contained the designer steroid Tetrahydrogestrinone (THG, or 'The Clear'), and the syringe would set in motion IRS special agent Jeff Novitzky's still on-going investigation into possible money laundering at BALCO, as well as the ultimate downfall of Conte, who would plead guilty to conspiracy to distribute steroids and spend four months in prison.

"Of particular interest to this case, Novitzky's investigation of BALCO's facilities uncovered an unsent letter, apparently written by Conte. The letter implied that Graham had been working with reputed steroid dealer and now star government witness Angel 'Memo' Heredia, who allegedly distributed steroids to over a dozen Olympic medalists, some of whom, including the disgraced Tim Montgomery, were coached by Graham. Heredia would later confirm the letter's assertion to federal investigators."

Thanks to the syringe Graham gave to the authorities, Don Catlin, director of the Olympic Analytical Laboratory in Los Angeles, was able to develop a testing process that made it possible to detect THG. He tested 550 samples from athletes, and 20 of them tested positive for THG.

In September 2003, Internal Revenue Service and U.S. Food and Drug Administration agents, together with the San Mateo Narcotics Task Force and the USADA, conducted a house search at BALCO. They found lists of customers as well as containers with labels identifying steroids and human growth hormones. At a search of Anderson's house they found cash, names, and dosage plans.

"The BALCO raid was the last day of unlawful activity from me," says Conte. "At the time I was doing what I was doing, I realized that there were risks attached with legal consequences. But I'm a big boy and I accepted the consequences. What I learned after that raid is that there are a large number of people that are harmed by your actions: your family and your friends. You don't just do the time in prison. Your family members and friends do as well. Going to prison is not the worst thing. It's when your family comes to visit you and you see the pain and suffering you have caused. They are not guilty of anything, yet they are devastated.

Victor Conte, founder of BALCO. Photo courtesy of Victor Conte.

"Athletes at BALCO made poor choices. They are not gods; they are people like everyone else. I feel worse about their family members. Those are the ones affected the most by what I did. Would I do it again? I would not. But at the same time I'm not the type of person to crawl under a rock and not come out again.

"In 2004 I decided to come public, and did it for all the right reasons. My legal counsel said I was nuts because I was convicting myself. I knew this going in. But I couldn't try to cut a deal for leniency. I felt that the world deserved to know the unadulterated truth about the rampant use of drugs over the last five decades. All the antidoping authorities were crawling under the table. Now here we are, four years later, and the world is a different place, isn't it?

"And we've personally seen what I call the boomerang effect that I find interesting. I made a decision to come forward and tell the truth. I spearheaded a plea bargain for the first four defendants who did our time and got out. I'm back out now with my life and business trying to redeem myself. The other ones are either in prison or headed there."

In July 2005 both Conte and Anderson agreed to plea bargains, pleading guilty to illegal steroid distribution and money laundering. Conte spent four months in prison; Anderson served more than a year in prison.

Another big break in the investigation occurred in December 2003, when former American League MVP Jason Giambi appeared before a grand jury and reportedly admitted using steroids and HGH. Giambi had asked Greg Anderson about the training regime of Barry Bonds and is believed to have begun his own regime. While he has never publicly admitted using steroids, Giambi has apologized for what he did.

Fainaru-Wada and Williams, the authors of *Game of Shadows*, were investigated in October 2006 and subpoenaed to appear before a grand jury to testify and identify the person who leaked Barry Bonds's name to them. After they refused to do so, federal prosecutors tried to have them jailed for up to eighteen months. But in February 2007, the charges were dropped when one of Conte's former attorneys, Troy Ellerman, admitted that he was the source of the leak and pleaded guilty to federal charges of unauthorized disclosure of grand jury testimony.

Barry Bonds, the home run king who was linked to BALCO, was indicted in November 2007 for perjury and obstruction of justice based on his grand jury testimony. His contract with the San Francisco Giants expired following the 2007 baseball season, and Bonds was not signed by another team.

The impact of Victor Conte and BALCO on the sports world is impossible to overstate. There are few areas of sport in which he has not had an effect.

"You'd have to say that he's had a pretty dramatic effect," says Fainaru-Wada. "In terms of strictly performance, all the athletes he dealt with were at the end of their careers and revitalized themselves and became better than they were in their careers. Football players are hard to quantify, but track stars and baseball players saw their statistics go through the roof. But another way he has had an effect is the level of consciousness there is now about the use of drugs in sports that people didn't realize before."

Conte is still in the nutrition business today. BALCO is no more, but he revived a supplement company he started in the 1980s, Scientific Nutrition for Advanced Conditioning (SNAC). He still works with a wide range of athletes, ranging from baseball players to weightlifters. His best-selling product is ZMA, a perfectly legal zinc-and-magnesium-based powder that helps athletes to repair tissue and sleep better.

"I was guilty and I paid the consequences, including going to prison," says Conte. "What I did was wrong, and I was punished.

When Marion Jones told all those lies and sued me for $25 million, I had to defend myself against her frivolous lawsuit. Then she had her tearful press conference in 2008 and she was exposed as a liar. The media came and asked me if I felt vindicated. I know what the truth is. I saw Marion's mother and her husband and realized that her children and others who cared about her were hurting. They didn't do anything wrong, but will still suffer greatly. I feel very sad."

Conte and SNAC are both doing very well. He has paid his dues to society and seems intent on trying to clean up the sports world. All these years later, Victor Conte is once again right where he likes to be: in the tower of power.

12

THE MITCHELL REPORT

Naming Names

"I never would have made it to the big leagues without them [steroids]. As a pitcher, if you throw 86 or 87 mph and you're not pretty perfect, you are going to get slayed. The hitters will kill you. At 95, you can make all kinds of mistakes and get away with it."

—Former Minnesota Twins and
New York Yankees pitcher Dan Naulty

By the time Major League Baseball hired former Senator George Mitchell to conduct an investigation into the use of steroids and other performance-enhancing drugs by big-league ballplayers, the problem was out of hand. Surely the game that its millions of fans had grown up with was nothing like the game had become. And the results of the investigation—the 409-page Mitchell Report—detailed in troubling terms just how serious the use of steroids and other illegal drugs had become in America's Pastime.

There was more than enough blame to be spread around. The players, their union, and baseball itself were all culpable. People on all sides of the equation had turned a blind eye to the numerous signs that there was a serious problem in Major League Baseball. Years of innuendo, questions, doubts, and sneaking suspicions were all proved true. Big-league ballplayers were juicing up and the game had become a bastardization of what it was supposed to be all about.

"This has not been an isolated problem involving just a few players or a few clubs," Mitchell said during a news conference shortly after the report was released. "Everyone involved in baseball over the past two decades—commissioners, club officials, the players association and players—share to some extent the responsibility for the steroids era. There was a collective failure to recognize the problem as it emerged and to deal with it early on."

The seriousness of the problem was not lost on the Mitchell Report: "For more than a decade there has been widespread illegal use of anabolic steroids and other performance enhancing substances by players in Major League Baseball, in violation of federal law and baseball policy. Club officials routinely have discussed the possibility of such substance use when evaluating players. Those who have illegally used these substances range from players whose major league careers were brief to potential members of the Baseball Hall of Fame. They include both pitchers and position players, and their backgrounds are as diverse as those of all major league players."

The twenty-one-month investigation resulted in the naming of more than 70 current and former major-league players who were implicated in the report. Mitchell was appointed to conduct the investigation on March 30, 2006, when baseball was reeling about revelations in the book *Game of Shadows*, which explained in great, troubling detail the extensive use of illegal drugs by players in general and Barry Bonds in particular. The Mitchell investigation was instituted after several members of Congress made negative comments about the effectiveness and honesty of the drug policies as well as the efforts by both the commissioner of Major League Baseball and the director of the players' union, Donald Fehr. The report, which was released on December 13, 2007, states that 5 to 7 percent of players tested positive for steroid use.

"It was very flattering that the commissioner of Baseball mentioned the book as a reason to start the investigation," says *Game of Shadows* coauthor Mark Fainaru-Wada. "Baseball has always been much more reactive than proactive. We were mentioned a lot in the Mitchell Report and we're very happy about that.

"We always felt confident in the work and that it could stand on its own and didn't need validation. But you still had doubters out there who thought we were making it up. But the mass of information has to weigh on the consciousness of any baseball fan. This is the

Mark Fainaru-Wada, coauthor of
Game of Shadows. Photo courtesy of
Mark Fainaru-Wada.

reality of the sport. If Senator Mitchell comes up with eighty-odd names, then clearly the use of drugs is widespread."

When mandatory random drug testing started in 2004, the new substance of choice for players then became human growth hormone, which was not detectable by tests. The report stated that the powerful Major League Baseball Players Association was largely uncooperative and actively discouraged players from cooperating with the investigation.

One of the major witnesses who cooperated in the investigation, Kirk Radomski, "provided substantial information about the distribution of performance enhancing substances." Radomski was a former clubhouse employee of the New York Mets who pleaded guilty to distributing anabolic steroids, human growth hormone, amphetamines, and other drugs to numerous players between 1995 and 2005. Many of the players named in the report were reported to be clients of Radomski's, including Chad Allen, Mike Bell, Gary Bennett, Larry Bigbie, Kevin Brown, Mark Carreon, Jason Christiansen, Howie Clark, Roger Clemens, Jack Cust, Brendan Donnelly, Chris Donnels, Lenny Dykstra, Matt Franco, Ryan Franklin, Éric Gagné, Jason Grimsley, Jerry Hairston Jr., Matt Herges, Phil Hiatt, Glenallen Hill, Todd Hundley, David Justice, Chuck Knoblauch, Tim Laker, Mike Lansing, Paul Lo Duca, Nook Logan, Josias Manzanillo, Cody McKay, Kent Mercker, Bart Miadich, Hal Morris, Denny Neagle, Jim Parque, Andy Pettitte, Adam Piatt, Todd Pratt, Stephen Randolph, Adam Riggs, Brian Roberts, F. P. Santangelo, David Segui, Mike Stanton, Miguel Tejada, Mo Vaughn, Ron Villone, Fernando Viña, Rondell White, Jeff Williams, Todd Williams, Kevin Young, and Gregg Zaun.

Also mentioned was Signature Pharmacy, which was alleged to have supplied illegal steroids and other substances to another group of players, including Rick Ankiel, Paul Byrd, Jay Gibbons, Troy Glaus, Jose Guillen, Jerry Hairston Jr., Gary Matthews Jr., Scott Schoeneweis, David Bell, José Canseco, Jason Grimsley, Darren Holmes, John Rocker, Ismael Valdéz, Matt Williams, and Steve Woodard. Another player identified in the report was former Minnesota Twins and New York Yankees pitcher Dan Naulty.

The group of players named represents some of the finest ballplayers in the last two decades. There are at least two bona fide Hall of Famers in Barry Bonds and Roger Clemens, as well as a number of All Star–caliber players. Many of those mentioned in the report have taken the high road and apologized for their lapse in judgment. One in particular, Naulty, has not only come clean about his own use, but has spoken out against steroid use in general and turned his life around.

During his four-year major-league career, the big right-hander boasted average MLB credentials for a relief pitcher. He was 5–5 with a 4.84 ERA in 130 games. His best season was his rookie year in Minnesota, when he went 3–2 in a career-high 49 games with a good 3.79 ERA. But the story of Dan Naulty goes a lot deeper than statistics.

Drafted in the fourteenth round of the amateur draft in 1992, he was an unspectacular pitcher who was not even considered a major-league prospect. He was throwing in the mid-80s with his fastball and was very thin, weighing in at 185 pounds.

"I got drafted in '92 by the Twins and was really thin coming out of college," Naulty says. "I was told to gain some weight because they thought I'd throw 100 mph since I was so tall. After my first season, I went to the local gym and hung out with the biggest guys in the room and they knew just what I wanted. I was implying that I wanted illegal drugs.

"I was using steroids for most of my career. I didn't use human growth hormone until my second-to-last year. I stopped quickly because it was very expensive. I injected steroids for about seven years. It was all very secretive. I think I only had one conversation openly about it out of all the years I played. Nobody talked about their steroid use. Some things were okay to talk about, but steroids weren't. Speed was common among the players. A high percentage used speed, and those were talked about very openly. I was mainly a

Dan Naulty credited steroid use for his making it to The Show. Photo courtesy of Minnesota Twins.

steroid user in the off-season and a speed user during the season. Then I became an alcoholic.

"It worked because I went from graduating college at 185 pounds and was at 240 three years later. And my fastball went from 86 or so to 95. As a result I went from a zero prospect in the Twins organization to a real prospect."

After four years in the minors, he quickly made it to The Show in his fifth season as a professional. A typical description of steroid use is that it doesn't help your performance; instead, steroids enable you to work out harder and recover more quickly, and, as a result, become much stronger. Naulty disagrees.

"You see an instantaneous result," he says. "I started taking steroids and was gaining a pound a day and had an immediate increase on my fastball. You'll hear people say that you can take all the drugs you want, but you still have to hit the ball and throw the ball. But once you do hit it, the ball will go farther, and you can throw harder because of increased velocity. All these athletes wouldn't be doing it if it didn't help performance.

"I never would have made it to the big leagues without them. As a pitcher, if you throw 86 or 87 mph and you're not pretty perfect, you are going to get slayed. The hitters will kill you. At 95, you can make all kinds of mistakes and get away with it."

Naulty continued to pitch fairly effectively and was traded to the New York Yankees prior to the start of the 1999 season. It was a year in which the Bronx Bombers were destined to capture the World Series crown. While he pitched well in New York, Naulty had some injuries as a direct result of his steroid use. And, it turned out, he'd had selective hearing about the dangers involved with use of such drugs.

"Well first off, as a user you don't necessarily delve into the consequences of using them," he says. "You hear about 'roid rage, but who cares? At that point, all I really knew about 'roid rage was what I was told by the people who were giving me my medical advice— drug users. They said if you only use them in the off-season like I did, at a four-month clip at a time, that I'd be okay.

"Before I got traded to New York, I had three really significant injuries in Minnesota, all related to my drug use. My third one was the most painful because I tore my big tendon in my groin off of my pelvis. I had too much muscle mass for my tendons, and they started tearing. After I tore my groin up, I decided that off-season to start taking growth hormone. I was taking it for the healing. That was my motive. I was plenty big enough at that point. It was still wrong and illegal, but that was my justification.

"That year in New York was the first year I played semi-clean. But toward the end of that year I realized I did so much damage to my body and also realized that I had done a lot of psychological harm to myself."

When Yankees closer Mariano Rivera got Keith Lockhart on a pop-up for the final out of their World Series win on October 27, 1999, Naulty celebrated and partied with his teammates. But he was in such a sorry state emotionally that he wanted to get out of a limo he and some of his friends were riding in—and jump off of the George Washington Bridge. The drugs had taken their toll, mentally as well as physically. And he was feeling a growing sense of guilt over how he achieved what most people consider the American Dream.

During his year with the Yankees, Naulty had some serious discussion with some of his teammates about life and Christianity. A number of the Christians on the team—including Scott Brosius, Andy Pettitte, Jason Grimsley, Joe Girardi, and Mariano Rivera—inspired him to devote his life to Christianity. While he decided that he was in no state, physically or emotionally, to play baseball again, his life finally took some positive turns.

"I remember riding across the George Washington Bridge talking to the limo driver about life," Naulty says. "The other guys were passed out in the backseat. I remember thinking that if this is supposed to be Nirvana, then I'm not even close.

"After that night I made a decision that I wanted to change my life. I was in the big leagues and successful, but I wasn't happy. But those guys gave me the chance to discuss Christianity and general life questions.

"So I chose a life change, and I don't miss it. I've often thought about whether I should have even played baseball, because I cheated my way all the way through. I never would have made it out of A Ball without the drugs and cheating. It's a tough thing, because baseball introduced me to my new life, but I had to go through all the misery to find it. I still enjoy watching baseball, but I don't miss the daily grind.

"I feel terrible about my career, because I railroaded so many guys that should have been ahead of me. Look at the damage I did to them. I was fortunate that God somehow used baseball to introduce me to him. But unfortunately, I made a lot of bad decisions and hurt a lot of people. My career is not satisfying because I did so much more damage than I did good."

These days, Dan Naulty has done a 180-degree turn. He went back to school to become an ordained minister and has pastored at a couple of churches in California. He got his first master's degree in biblical studies and his second in theological studies. Currently he is seeking his PhD in theology and has been accepted into Oxford.

But not all of the drug users outed in the Mitchell Report in baseball have made the turnaround that Naulty has. The torrid stream of information from books such as *Game of Shadows*, as well as the Mitchell Report and the BALCO scandal, has forced users out of the drug closet and into the open. Stiffer testing by Major League

Baseball and other sports will make it harder for athletes to cheat at this level again. But still the battle rages and the denials continue.

Plainly, baseball needs to do more to effectively address this problem. As Jeff Kent of the Los Angeles Dodgers said in September, as reported in several newspapers: "Major League Baseball is trying to investigate the past so they can fix the future."

There is no doubt in the wording of the Mitchell Report as to what needs to be done to clean up Major League Baseball:

"That is the purpose of the recommendations that are set forth in detail in this report. In summary, they fall into three categories: (1) Major League Baseball must significantly increase its ability to investigate allegations of use outside of the testing program and improve its procedures for keeping performance enhancing substances out of the clubhouse; (2) there must be a more comprehensive and effective program of education for players and others about the serious health risks incurred by users of performance enhancing substances; and (3) when the club owners and the Players Association next engage in collective bargaining on the joint drug program, I urge them to incorporate into the program the principles that characterize a state-of-the-art program, as described in this report."

Perhaps the greatest talent of his generation, Barry Bonds has seen literally all of his accomplishment in the game questioned because of his alleged drug use, which is supposedly rooted in his jealousy over the attention given Mark McGwire during his chase of Roger Maris's single-season home run record. He has repeatedly denied ever knowingly using steroids, despite the evidence outlined in *Game of Shadows*. He has been indicted on five counts of perjury and obstruction of justice, charges stemming from a federal probe that examined his alleged use of steroids.

Bonds has seen his status diminish from one of the great natural talents in the history of the game to a universally disliked—and even hated—player who used artificial methods to become baseball's home run king, eclipsing the great Hank Aaron. The only park where Bonds was universally cheered was at home in San Francisco. But after the 2007 season and the indictments, Bonds was not tendered a contract offer by the Giants—or any other major league team.

Under oath, Bonds said that he was told that a cream given him by his trainer, Greg Anderson, was flaxseed oil. Federal prosecutors will seek to prove that the purported flaxseed oil was actually illegal substances supplied by BALCO, known as "the Clear" and "the Cream."

"It's his statement and he's sticking to it," says Fainaru-Wada. "And he's under indictment for lying to the feds. The government clearly doesn't believe he's telling the truth. He was taking a wide range of substances, including injectables. I don't think you inject flaxseed oil. He's also not the first guy to talk about taking drugs and supposedly not knowing it. Several people involved with BALCO said the same thing."

According to the indictment, during the criminal investigation, evidence—including positive tests for the presence of anabolic steroids and other performance-enhancing substances for Bonds and other athletes—was obtained.

Regardless of one's opinion of Bonds, his attitude toward the press and fans, or his alleged use of performance-enhancing drugs, his fall from grace and favor is a tragic result of baseball's drug scandal. No matter what happens to him, he remains the all-time home run king in Major League Baseball. As was the case when Roger Maris eclipsed the single-season home run record of Babe Ruth, there is much discussion as to whether or not this record should include an asterisk.

"I draw the line there," says Don Hooton, whose son Taylor, a high school baseball player, committed suicide as he attempted to stop his steroid use. "Asterisks? What he committed was a felony. How did we get into a discussion about if steroid use is cheating or not? This is a felony. We should be asking how many years in the penitentiary these people are going to get, not if there will be an asterisk after a record. How did we get sucked into these debates?"

Another star who has seen his glory fade quickly is Roger Clemens, also named in the Mitchell Report. A twenty-four-year major-league veteran, Clemens has pitched for Boston, Toronto, Houston and the New York Yankees, amassing 354 victories and 4,672 strikeouts during his illustrious career. He's won twenty games four times and won seven Cy Young Awards.

But the former flame-throwing right-hander was implicated by his former trainer of ten years, Brian McNamee, who claims he injected Clemens with human growth hormone at least sixteen times over a period of several years. Clemens's best friend in the game and former workout partner, fellow pitcher Andy Pettitte, admitted that he used human growth hormone while rehabbing from an injury and said that he thought Clemens admitted drug use to him.

But Clemens has gone on the offensive, bitterly, strongly, and pointedly denying that he ever used any type of performance-enhancing drug. While McNamee has a spotty past and may not be considered credible, Pettitte is considered an honest, good person, causing his assertion to carry more weight.

Clemens appeared before Congress and even was interviewed by Mike Wallace on the television news show *60 Minutes*. At every step, he has continued to deny any sort of drug use.

The FBI and IRS are investigating whether or not Clemens lied in front of a congressional committee on February 13, 2008, about his drug use. The former pitcher has also filed a defamation suit against McNamee, who kept various drug paraphernalia that he claims Clemens used to inject steroids, such as syringes and bloody gauze pads, saying that the traces of DNA will prove that he is telling the truth and that Clemens is lying.

In an unfortunate side occurrence, Clemens's credibility took a strong hit when rumors of extramarital affairs with Mindy McCready, Angela Moyer, and Paulette Dean Daly, the former wife of golfer John Daly, were made public.

"Just because you are a phenomenal pitcher does not mean you are a smart person," says author Jerrold Casway. "You could be an athletic icon and still be an idiot."

One of the real debates that has come from the drug era in sports in general and baseball in particular is what, if anything, should be done with the records that have fallen by the wayside. If Barry Bonds is never convicted and never admits using steroids, his home run record is undeniable. But if he is guilty, does an asterisk go next to his records?

In track and field, records of doped athletes are erased, but baseball does not do that, because it would be impossible to even attempt to substantiate just how many extra home runs, wins, or strikeouts a player got because of an illegal advantage.

"There are eras in the game when it's just goofy," says Williams. "The ball is juiced and guys are hitting way more home runs than they should be. I think we'll look back on this ten-year period as an aberration, like the game wasn't really normal, and think about the records in the context that they were set. People who care about the game and its returning to the planet Earth will look at this era and take the steroids into account.

"In baseball, the change comes the time when weight training is suddenly okay after a century of no weight training. Hank Aaron was forbidden from lifting weights. When they started lifting, that's when you had these guys getting the exposure to steroids. José Canseco says he is the Typhoid Mary of steroids in baseball, and maybe he is."

The allegations and headlines have changed the way we look at sports. It's impossible not to have a more jaded view of sports and those who play them. And that's unfortunate, when you consider the vast majority of players are honest athletes who don't dope.

"I look at sports in a much different way than I used to," admits Fainaru-Wada. "I think I have more open eyes about what sports are and what they mean and what they represent. It hasn't made me less of a baseball fan, or less of a football fan, or less of a basketball fan. These athletes are unbelievable, whether they are taking drugs or not. But I must say that I'm much more skeptical than I was."

13

THE END OF GAMES

The Taylor Hooton Tragedy

"I just hope and pray that Taylor's life wasn't lost in vain and that through our loss and our example that Taylor becoming the face of this problem can take it out of the realm of the asterisks and get it focused where it needs to be—on our children."

—Don Hooton

"The youth of this country and other countries model their behavior after prominent athletes. Athletes are second only to parents in the extent to which they are admired by children. If Major League Baseball players send a message that the illegal use of performance enhancing drugs is acceptable, more young athletes will use these substances as they emulate these prominent figures."

—The Mitchell Report

Perhaps the most gripping, serious passages from the Mitchell Report deal not with which athletes used what drugs and when, but with the trickle-down effect of steroid use by professional and world-class amateur athletes on the young athletes who want so desperately to follow in their footsteps. We certainly can empathize with the families and loved ones of a professional athlete who makes the decision to risk his or her life by taking steroids and other performance-enhancing drugs. But they are mature adults who make those decisions, weighing the risks versus the rewards. Many have had their lives drastically altered by such use, while some, in fact, have lost their lives.

But when high school–aged kids risk their futures and their lives by imitating the same misguided behavior, it's time to make that aforementioned invisible line of acceptable behavior much more visible. Studies indicate that one in twenty high school students is taking or has taken these products. Considering that there are approximately 17 million high school students in the United States, that translates to anywhere from eight hundred thousand to 1 million high school kids using steroids. To be blunt, if a thirty-year-old dies as a result of using performance-enhancing drugs, it is the result of the choice made by a mature adult old enough to make life decisions. We all make mistakes in life. But when teenagers lose their lives because of bad decisions involving the effects of such drug use, the time for action is long overdue. There needs to be accountability.

"Our battle is not about a thirty-year-old man who has decided to take steroids," says Don Hooton, whose seventeen-year-old son, Taylor, killed himself in 2003, in a state of depression brought about by withdrawal from the use of steroids. "But what is the issue is that they are role models and have a responsibility to be a good example for our kids.

"I don't care if world-class athletes want to be role models or not. They *are* role models. Period. We, as citizens and fans, need to be holding these guys accountable. Look at the Bash Brothers out in Oakland back in the day. We stood in the stands and cheered and revenues went up. So we rewarded the behavior. We certainly as customers didn't send a signal to Major League Baseball or to the players that we didn't like the behavior. We sent the opposite message.

"It was a big joke, and that's where we got ourselves into trouble. If you take it just on the level of cheating, we all just winked right along with Canseco, McGwire, and Bonds. We rewarded it with record ticket sales. And in fairness, it wasn't just baseball. It was other sports. It was football, cycling, and even golf now."

There is no doubt that this is not just baseball's problem. All sports have been touched, in one fashion or another, by the use of drugs to improve performance. But in large part as a result of the Mitchell Report, baseball has finally taken the lead in awareness and prevention. It's only fair because, like it or not, cyclists don't normally adorn a cereal box, nor do swimmers, weightlifters, discus throwers, or many other Olympic athletes. But baseball is America's Pastime, and the incredible depth of the use of steroids and other drugs by baseball players has touched literally every scholastic athlete in the country. Who hasn't heard about the questions surrounding the likes of Barry Bonds, Mark McGwire, Rafael Palmeiro, et al.? Far too often, the focus is narrow, while it should be much wider and much younger.

As the Mitchell Report stated: "After the Associated Press reported in August 1998 that Mark McGwire was using androstenedione, a steroid precursor that was legal at the time, sales of that supplement increased by over 1,000%. McGwire may not have wanted to be a role model, but he was.

"According to the National Institute on Drug Abuse, by 2001, 8% of male high school seniors had used andro within the prior year. Some estimates appear to show a recent decline in steroid use by high school students; they range from 3 to 6 percent. But even the lower figure means that hundreds of thousands of high school–aged young people are still illegally using steroids."

"Ballplayers like to say that they are not a role model and I agree that they should not be looked at as examples of how to live your life," says Lance Williams, coauthor of *Game of Shadows*. "But elite athletes always will be role models to young athletes. The real problem with introducing steroids into the high school scene is that every kid on every prep or little league team is pretty darn sure that he will play in the big leagues, which, of course, isn't true. A minuscule number will make it. But many of their parents feel that it will happen as well. If you convince them that the route to that success is steroids, you will have lots of kids with no chance of making it messing themselves up."

Again, to quote the Mitchell Report: "It's important to devote attention to the Major League Baseball players who illegally used performance enhancing substances. It's at least as important, perhaps even more so, to be concerned about the reality that hundreds of thousands of our children are using them. Every American, not just baseball fans, ought to be shocked into action by that disturbing truth."

Young people rarely understand the tenuous nature of life: just how fragile a gift it is. When you're young, you feel as if you will live forever. Young people often don't fully understand the effects of their actions. They have a feeling of immortality, which, unfortunately, is no more realistic for teenagers than it is for anyone else. But there are times when good kids with a seemingly bright future lose it all by making ill-advised decisions.

While there are, sadly, too many examples, perhaps the most well-known case of a young athlete paying the ultimate price for trying to get that little edge is that of Taylor Hooton. The cousin of former major-league pitcher Burt Hooton, Taylor was a pitcher at West Senior High School in Plano, Texas. He had size, at six-foot-two and 180 pounds, a baseball pedigree, and a hard-breaking curveball. But to become the big-time hurler he so wanted to be, a high school coach suggested that he needed to grow.

While the coach in question apparently did not give him any training regimen or diet to help him achieve that goal, Taylor Hooton began taking illegal steroids, sometimes stealing to get the money he needed to purchase the chemicals necessary to build up. And build up he did. Hooton gained thirty pounds, but along with the added muscle, he got severe acne on his back and increasing instances of 'roid rage. He changed from the pleasant, even-keeled young man that everyone in Plano knew to a big guy with a short temper.

Taylor Hooton was changing his body—his physiology—by injecting himself with steroids three times a week as well as taking pills, a practice known as stacking. His parents noticed a difference in their son and took him to a psychiatrist, who found out that Taylor had been using and abusing steroids. The psychiatrist got him to quit using steroids, with the help of his family, and prescribed an antidepressant. His initial reaction seemed very promising. The Hootons thought that they had their fine young man back.

"We thought we had dodged another bullet," says Don Hooton. "Taylor admitted what he was doing and stopped. But what none of us knew at the time is that when a user stops using steroids, depending on how much he took, how long he took, and what he took, that the body has stopped producing testosterone. Here you have a seventeen-year-old kid with his body producing no testosterone. But we didn't know that. But worst of all, the doctor didn't know that. As a result we are working with the American College of Sports Medicine to get scientists to give a treatment regime to help athletes get off steroids.

Don Hooton (left)
with his late son,
Taylor. Photo
courtesy of
Don Hooton.

"Taylor was in another continuation of bad behavior. In the spring he had some issues, and then he stole some stuff from the hotel while we were vacationing in Europe. After our return we sat down as a family and had an intervention with him—no yelling or screaming or anything like that. It was me and his mom, [and] his brother and sister, who all sat down at the kitchen table and we all told Taylor we loved him. But that this time he had gone over the line. The whole family was in England, and we could have been in jeopardy. What we wound up doing was we grounded him for two weeks [when the family returned home]. Kids have been grounded for two weeks for a lot less.

"The next morning, Taylor got up and begged his mom to please not ground him. He said he'd sign a contract or anything we liked. My wife told him that he did something really serious and that he could talk to his pop that night when I got home. He went up into his room and hung himself. It's been five years, and my wife has never gone back to where she found him."

There are many ways to remember a fallen child, but perhaps the one with the most honor and integrity is to try to ensure that no other child has to face the same fate. And that is just what the Hooton family has done. The memory of their son and the kind of kid he was has helped the family deal with their enormous loss.

"There are no words to describe it," says Hooton. "You talk about it enough and enough time goes by, and it is a healing therapy. If talking about what happened is therapy, then I've had as much therapy as you can possibly have.

"Taylor was a great kid. He had a wonderful personality. If he walked into a room and saw you talking to me, he'd walk right up to you, look in your eyes, give you a firm handshake, and introduce himself. He was very confident around adults, and a good-looking kid too. I used to kid him and say, 'For you the girls [are] like a bus; there will be another one along in fifteen minutes.' He carried a 3.8 grade point average in school. Over three thousand people came to his funeral. He was just an all around good kid."

In February 2004, just seven months after Taylor's death, the Taylor Hooton Foundation was formed, with Don Hooton filling the post of president. The nonprofit organization is chartered with the purpose of attacking the issue of youth performance-enhancing drug use.

"Why do we exist?" asks Hooton. "Our vision is to reach the day when performance-enhancing drugs will no longer be a part of our high school students' lives. In short, we are trying to eliminate the performance-enhancing drug problem from our schools. We are this nation's first private organization to take on this problem. We are recognized as a leader in this battle. For example, when any major news organization is looking for input on this topic, we are almost always at the top of their contact list.

"Our organization is built on a set of values: honesty, integrity, fair play, and healthy competition. We teach kids that there are ways to achieve their objectives by doing it the right way—with proper exercise, diet, and hard work."

To accomplish these goals, the Taylor Hooton Foundation has implemented a number of programs. The organization's goal is to be recognized as the premier place on the Internet that people can visit to obtain accurate, complete, and up-to-date information related to performance-enhancing drugs.

The foundation also reaches out to kids with the Hoot's Chalk Talks program. During these programs staff members and guest speakers talk to kids and parents about the dangers of steroids—physically and psychologically. Then, they show the kids how to achieve their goals naturally, without the use of drugs. Finally, they regularly have a law enforcement agent with them who speaks about the legal risk users take when they decide to use steroids without a prescription. One of the major elements of the program is when they tell the kids, "If you haven't listened to anything else we've told you during this program, listen to the guy with the badge and the gun, because you can spend time in jail if you get caught with this junk."

To date, the Taylor Hooton Foundation has had representatives speak to well over thirty thousand students, parents, and coaches across America. These programs have been held in venues ranging from high school auditoriums to Major League Baseball parks. They have addressed large groups of doctors, civic groups, Olympic athletes, and others. Members of the organization have spoken to virtually anyone who will listen and that combined with a large number of media programs have helped them to reach tens of millions of Americans with their messages—all built upon Taylor's story.

How big is the performance-enhancing drug problem? Most experts agree that about a million high school students have taken anabolic steroids as of 2007, and that number increases each year. In fact, the fastest-growing user group is young girls! "This stuff is all around us—and our kids are buying this junk locally," says Hooton. "Taylor met his dealer at our neighborhood YMCA."

What's it going to take to solve this problem? As a starting point, it will take America waking up and realizing that we really have a problem here. Parents and coaches everywhere have to begin by admitting that this is a problem that is going on in their children's school, on their children's team, and maybe even in their children's bedroom. This will require a real national effort. It can't be done alone, which is why groups like the Taylor Hooton Foundation and their partners have become so important.

"We want to take our Hoot's Chalk Talks program to every major high school in this country," says Hooton. "We want role models to accompany us to speak at these high schools. To that end, we are in discussions with a number of athletic organizations in hopes that many of their athletes and medalists can join us when we meet with kids.

"Sadly, the reality is that many of our parents, coaches, and teachers are still not fully aware of the dangers our kids face from steroids. When I ask kids whether their leaders are talking with them about the dangers of steroids, it is rare that more than 10 percent of hands go up."

In addition to Hoot's Chalk Talks, the foundation is challenging the remaining forty-nine states to pass Taylor's Law, the law passed in Texas in June 2007 that calls for random steroid testing of high school students participating in extracurricular activities.

The foundation would also like to find some high-profile professional and elite athletes to speak out and let the kids know that there are athletes who stand against the use of drugs in sports, because the silence from the good guys has been deafening. The foundation is hoping to put together public service announcements to be aired on TV and radio stations across the country in which sports idols deliver messages directly to kids—letting them know that they've achieved their success without drugs. The foundation's first PSA features NFL legend Dick Butkus and his son Matt.

The foundation has made a great deal of progress with a small team plus a number of volunteers. Taylor's story is a gut-wrenching tale of a fine young man who got mixed up with drugs, made some bad decisions, and paid the ultimate price. And, like so many others, he took drugs not as an escape or to get high, but because he thought they'd improve his chances of making the starting lineup on his varsity baseball team. There is little doubt he thought that this was an okay way to get there, because he saw so many of his idols and his peers following this path.

Regardless of how much progress the foundation makes, their efforts are hampered by elite athletes who continue to set a poor example for our children. These drugs are readily available to our children, and coaches still have not been motivated to really step up to solve this problem.

"But I remain optimistic," says Hooton. "I can visualize the programs and the steps that need to be taken to eliminate these drugs from our schools. We are dealing with good kids, our best kids, in fact. And I am convinced that with proper education and good role models that this is one drug problem that we can beat. And we are prepared to be that voice—to educate our children to make a difference in their culture and in their lives.

"While standing on the porch of the funeral home after Taylor's wake, I commented to our friend, 'What is this awful thing, and why isn't anyone talking about it?' It was then that I realized that God had given me the gift that no one would ever want. And that is because I lost my son to steroids I have been given the assignment to speak out and to lead the effort to rid our country of this terrible scourge.

"We've done our best to fill that void over the past years, and we will continue to lead this charge into the future."

The Taylor Hooton foundation has found many benefactors over the years, and one of the most supportive has been Major League Baseball. In August 2008, MLB announced that it would provide $1.5 million and other forms of support to the Taylor Hooton Foundation as part of an aggressive grassroots antisteroid education program.

MLB was a founding sponsor of the foundation in August 2005, initially providing a $1 million contribution. The new agreement extends the commitment to 2011. MLB will continue to encourage all major- and minor-league clubs to support and promote the Taylor Hooton Foundation. A Web site devoted to information about the foundation will be created in the community section of MLB.com and also will include a link to the Taylor Hooton Foundation Web site. MLB will also allow the use of its logo on the Web site and its other educational and promotional materials.

"Major League Baseball has been thoroughly impressed by the work of the Taylor Hooton Foundation since our alliance began three years ago," says MLB Commissioner Bud Selig. "Don Hooton's leadership in the fight against steroids and performance enhancing substances has been inspiring. Major League Baseball's collaboration with the Taylor Hooton Foundation is an important component of our extensive overall efforts to support awareness, education and research. We look forward to expanding our relationship with the Taylor Hooton Foundation."

The Taylor Hooton tragedy represents the worst possible scenario to result from the use of steroids and other performance-enhancing substances. Impressionable young athletes who dream of professional careers are literally putting their lives on the line. If a coach tells a player to "beef up," that advice should be followed with a closely monitored weight-training program. It is a naive and potentially tragic path to take without close interaction between the coach and player.

It is also incredibly naive to assume that youngsters can't access these drugs, even in the nicest of neighborhoods. If the horrible ending to Taylor Hooton's life can serve a purpose and keep a similar tragedy from happening to other teenagers, his death and the efforts of his father and the Taylor Hooton Foundation will have meaning.

But his death is a tragic waste.

14

THE BIG FIX

Fixing Society . . . Not Just Sports

"I think we cheat because we don't believe we belong to each other. In some places there is a greater sense of connection, and I would expect less cheating there. The way we show we know we belong to each other in a competitive society is to play by the rules. In our culture, we honor innovation—building a better mousetrap through ingenuity and hard work. We do not honor cheating, which is breaking the rules which are there for the common good."

—Pastor Mike Wicks

Unless they make their living as a bookie, a numbers runner, or a latter-day Arnold Rothstein, just about everyone is in agreement that the sports world needs the big fix. No, it doesn't need another fix such as a thrown World Series or another crooked NBA official (or officials), and it certainly doesn't need another steroid scandal. It needs a fix in the sense of healing—making things right in the sports world. Isn't it time for athletes to stop going over that imaginary line and play the games by the rules? For the fans, wouldn't it be refreshing to enjoy a contest of some sort with absolutely no thought that anything questionable could be going on? We could take a step back in time to a kinder, gentler era, with black-and-white television and Jim McKay hosting *The Wide World of Sports* on a Saturday afternoon.

Of course, even in those days, there was cheating going on as well. While cleansing sports seems a lofty goal, the sports world is not the lone culprit in this world full of cheats and sleazes. Cheating and other dishonest behavior goes on in every part of our lives, and the United States is certainly not the only country saddled with these problems. But you've got to start somewhere.

"Fix American morality?" asks Maury Allen "I don't think you can. There is a percentage of people who go into every business, whether it's the stock market, sales, or sports, who will distort and change the rules to benefit themselves. I think we're just not the same moral country we were before the Vietnam War, and I don't see any signs of that changing."

Even if the desire to change the way we think and act is honestly there, it's nearly impossible to try to act as a conscience for the masses or create a conscience for them. Each and every one of us knows what we see each time we look into a mirror. It starts with each one of us.

We certainly can't look to our political leaders for guidance. They've proven to be totally incapable as moral beacons in our lives. Religion? For every person who finds a particular religious group or leader to be a light at the end of life's tunnel, there is another person who considers it a crock. So where do we look to try to make the world in general, and our sports world in particular, a better, more honest place?

The first place we have to look is within ourselves. Before we can expect anyone else to act with honor and dignity, we have to take the lead ourselves. It's easy to expect others to take us down the path of morality and good living. But as we've learned over and over again, the loudest speakers on the tallest soapboxes often live in houses made of the most breakable glass. But if a better world and more honorable athletic competition is what you truly desire, it has to start with each and every one of us individually. We must stop teaching our children to cheat at very young ages. We must be good, strong parents who stand up and refuse to allow any sort of cheating in our kids. That kind of parenting takes time and effort and is extremely difficult. But as stated in the first chapter by Kirk O. Hanson, little cheating can easily turn into big cheating.

Those who seem to understand our challenges point to ideas such as community and trusting others. They champion the idea that we really aren't alone as we traverse down life's path. That thought process is not for everyone, but it has worked for many who looked for some kind of guidance and comfort in their lives.

"One of the reasons we cheat is that we feel we are facing the challenges of life all alone," says Pastor Mike Wicks. "If managing the slings and arrows of outrageous fortune is all up to us by ourselves, then what difference does it make if I cheat the grocery store out of some of its profit? We are a highly competitive society. I think we cheat because we don't believe we belong to each other. In some places there is a greater sense of connection and I would expect less cheating there.

"The way we show we know we belong to each other in a competitive society is to play by the rules. In our culture, we honor innovation— building a better mousetrap through ingenuity and hard work. We do not honor cheating, which is breaking the rules which are there for the common good. The butcher who mixes horse meat in with his ground beef to improve the profit margin illustrates this wolf in sheep's clothing, or, if you will, cheating in the clothing of innovation.

"I bet the first time someone threw a spitball in baseball they thought it was an innovation on a standard pitch. Pine tar on the bat is only cheating if everyone can't do it. I suspect steroids appeared to be an innovation for better fitness on the part of those who use them. Who decides where the line is in the contract we have with one another in the community, be we butchers, bakers, or ballplayers? The line is much harder to see if we don't believe we have any kind of connection with each other at all to begin with. If all we are is competitors, then any innovation which helps us will appear as a good thing. If we know we belong to each other, even when we are competing in the marketplace, or on the fields of sports competition, there will be limits and lines we are not willing to cross."

So we police ourselves because, in a larger sense, we are all part of the same ballclub, even though we compete on a regular basis in all the innings of our lives. But if everyone is not on board with that idea and the shared commitment to those ideals, it becomes rather difficult to see to its fruition. Much like in the nuclear freeze debate of the 1980s, it only takes one country to go back on its word to make the whole idea a tragic example of a naive yet well-meaning concept.

Doing the right thing in private is one thing, but acting properly in public can be a difficult exercise, where you can expect marginal response at best. Just because you choose to live your life in an honest, moral way doesn't necessarily convince your neighbor down the street to live his or her life in a similar manner.

"You will be swimming upstream given the culture today," says Hanson. "But there are rewards from swimming upstream. Happiness—true happiness—does not occur from getting ahead by cheating. Happiness comes from doing your best and being part of a community, be it a family or neighborhood. Those things are often made more difficult by overachievement. The person who comes out number one and brags like hell to his family and friends is not the most loved family member and neighbor. But part of it is that one gets a new sense of what constitutes happiness.

"Happiness may counteract the feeling of getting ripped off. The younger generation seems to have an antenna about this problem. People are destroying themselves to get ahead. They tie themselves in knots trying to focus on being number one. But the price you pay may be so high and the end result may not be the happiness you sought.

"I think that our families are caught in the cultural bind of feeling a failure if they are not rich. But they can give that signal of how happy you can be by just being yourself, rather than the relentless pursuit of wealth or getting ahead."

Look at all the pitfalls that enter the equation with cheating. The entire concept leads to a "Cheating Society," where some people cheat to get ahead and others cheat just trying to keep up and get their piece of the pie. Since we're all human, we're all tempted to cheat. And as Wicks insists, cheating weakens the trust between ourselves and all those around us. How can you be genuinely friendly with other parents when they encourage their kids to cheat in Little League? How can they trust you if your child bends the rules with your blessing? Is it even possible to have a healthy, trusting work environment where employees stab each other in the back, or run roughshod over a coworker's protected sales territory? Cheating creates an atmosphere of distrust and of selfishness, quite the contrary of what community is supposed to be all about.

There is also another aspect of cheating that is easy to forget: It costs more when people cheat. When people cheat, it means our security measures are not up to the challenge, creating the necessity for larger expenditures to catch the dishonest among us. Upgraded security and surveillance systems and measures like drug testing do not come cheaply. But we are increasingly seeing the need to ramp up our self-policing.

If we want to fix the sports world and eliminate as much cheating as is possible, our entire society first needs to be fixed. It is, no doubt, an immense project that may well be worth the effort. Perhaps increased scrutiny of our day-to-day lives—better parenting that includes penalties for dishonest behavior, and less acceptance of "little" cheating at home, in school, and at work—would help. But a new sense of self-awareness about what we need for our own happiness would be helpful as well.

"A number of happiness studies have been done and happiness ain't advancement," says Hanson. "Once you have the basic comforts, happiness comes more from integrity than advancement.

"There is an ever-present temptation to cheat. People don't look over our shoulder every second in sports [or] in life. Most of the cheating never comes to public light. So it's only in our souls that we judge whether it was worth it. And this is very closely tied to what we think a worthwhile life is. If we define it as wealth and getting ahead, we will treat cheating differently. I'm in favor of drug testing and monitoring people. It's to help people who are tempted to cheat and need one more reason not to do it."

Another possible roadblock to acting dishonestly and cheating could be a belief in God and maintaining a solid religious foundation. Obviously this is not something that everyone agrees upon, but it is a viable consideration when discussing proper behavior in society. If there is some kind of a divine payday at the end of life's long and winding road, the rules and mores we so often struggle with might be easier to live with and worth the effort. Of course, a belief in God is not the end-all answer. While for some it does give a moral roadmap for life, it is not only nonbelievers who cheat, and not only believers who refrain from cheating.

"If we belong to each other because we belong to God, then not playing fair in life, however we define that, is more than just a slick way to get ahead," says Wicks. "It is a violation of our common bond and a slap in the face to God, who gives us to each other.

"When God gives us the Ten Commandments in Exodus 20, he starts by saying, 'I am the Lord your God.' The ethical imperatives are rooted in spiritual connectedness—to God and to each other. We cheat more when we believe this less. Do religious people cheat? Sure, because they are people. But when we know we belong to God and to each other, because when we believe the structures which create the rules are meaningful and right, we are going to be less inclined to violate those relationships."

Jennifer DiStefano the student assistance coordinator for Cherry Hill, New Jersey, public schools also sees the importance of some sort of religious guide in our lives to help keep us honest. Again, it's not for everyone but it offers one more reason not to act in a dishonest manner. "I think that cheating is wrong and that it compromises your moral values," she says. "More and more families are falling away from religious beliefs that include moral teachings."

But religion isn't the only answer, and it's not the answer for everyone. It remains an age-old existential question in our culture today. If you believe in God and an afterlife, your behavior on Earth will have a profound affect on your acceptance into heaven—or whatever your idea of an afterlife might be. Not only do you obey the rules of society, but you have a higher code of ethics that you need to be followed to earn the ultimate afterlife payoff.

But what is expected of those who don't believe in a Supreme Being? Other than the fear of societal punishment, what motives do *they* have to be trusting and trusted members of the community at large?

Perhaps the answer is the simple realization that it's better to do things the right way. Much like the old saying that the journey is more important than the ultimate destination, it is the struggle to be the best we can be that will ultimately win this moral tug-of-war and enable more of us to simply enjoy the ride. It is fighting the temptation to take the easy or dishonest way that makes victory even sweeter. Whether you become a champion or not, giving a championship effort and leaving nothing in the clubhouse is something to be proud of, particularly if your efforts were all aboveboard and honest.

While many reputations have been soiled by the use of performance-enhancing drugs in sports, it is important to remember that the large majority of athletes do not cheat, do not use steroids, and do not cross that invisible line that separates proper conduct from cheating. The revelations of athletes who cheat will continue to make headlines until a new attitude prevails in sports and in society.

As for the sports world, testing has increased and improved, but you can rest assured that at this very moment there is, somewhere, a latter-day Patrick Arnold trying to invent a new, designer performance-enhancing drug that will slip through the current testing structure. And while many watchdog groups and antidoping authorities and agencies continue to assure us that things are better now and that sports are much cleaner than they have been, that may or may not be the case.

Victor Conte's influence on sports was detailed in earlier chapters. But now that his days of trying to beat the system are over, the founder of BALCO is trying to fix the system. He is not thrilled with what he sees.

"Some antidoping people consider me helpful, but others think of me as a thorn in their side," Conte says. "I believe that they are still attempting to sweep a lot of this history under the rug and are not 'fessing up that the antidoping procedures to this day are very inept. They have a test for growth hormone that is basically worthless.

"In terms of designer steroids, post-BALCO there are none. Tests can in fact detect something similar in structure to a designer steroid which they will detect. But there is fast-acting testosterone that can clear from your system in less than a day. Antidoping authorities will argue that if they have a tip that someone is using, that they have tests that can differentiate. But it costs about $500, as opposed to the regular testing which is $50. So they rarely use it.

"They need to concentrate their testing out of competition during the fourth quarter of the year. This is the off-season for athletes, and it's the time when they use anabolic steroids to build the explosive strength base that serves them throughout the competitive season. Now they test the top one-hundred-ranked athletes in the world twice a year out of competition. Forget the rest and just test the top twenty five times and concentrate during the fourth quarter, or off-season, when they're using anabolic steroids. But testing in the fourth quarter has been cut in half.

"You don't do that. You don't reduce the total amount of tests in the fourth quarter. That's like a fisherman sitting at a pond and when the fish start biting, he decides to reel in the fishing line, put on his straw hat and take a nap."

Whether or not our society will be guilty of taking such a nap is yet to be seen. There are many reasons for concern out there. But for every crooked politician, dishonest cop, or pervert who preys on the young, there are countless others who dedicate their lives to doing the right thing, who act with honor and discipline, serving their fellow people. Yes, there are reasons for serious concern in our society—but there are also reasons to celebrate.

Our culture needs a positive attitude of victory. It's easy to look at the negative side of any equation or life situation and expect the worst to happen. But in the sports world, just as in society, the good far outweighs the bad. That contest isn't even close.

There are positive role models out there, in all areas of life, doing what is right. Countless coaches are working with kids—the athletes of the future—teaching them right from wrong. Winning is important, but developing people is their primary focus.

"We try to follow the rules," said high school coach Bob Shelton. "I just feel like if I personally did something I know in my heart was wrong, that I couldn't handle it. The pressure of winning is not going to bother me enough to do something illegal to win. We will work as hard as we can to win. My staff has been together since 1994, and we do things the right way and we feel we can win the right way.

"I've followed athletics my whole life, and I knew from an early age that whatever I did would involve athletics. Some people are driven in that direction. Coaching is something I was born to do. You see the cheating and you know it's going on. The thing that is hard is if you know somebody else is doing it, the temptation is to do it yourself."

The worst thing that can happen is for the masses of sports fans to give in to cynicism. We as fans should not ever assume that because someone does something remarkable on a field of play, he or she was anything less than honest and aboveboard. Succeeding does not necessarily mean cheating, and in America, we are innocent until proven guilty. Roger Clemens has had his name and reputation muddied by allegations relating to performance-enhancing drugs as well as his personal behavior. He has lashed out at his accusers, loudly and forcefully proclaiming his innocence. But because so many athletes have disappointed us in recent times, many people treated Clemens as guilty until proven innocent.

That's wrong. At the end of his *60 Minutes* interview with Mike Wallace, Clemens said, "Twenty-four, twenty-five years, Mike. You'd think I'd get an inch of respect. An inch."

Clemens deserves the benefit of the doubt. If he is eventually proven guilty, he deserves whatever happens. But the world can't act as judge and jury before all the evidence is in. It's simply not right. And if there isn't enough evidence, then he is innocent. And what if he truly *is* innocent? What if he never used steroids, human growth hormone, or anything other than Bayer Aspirin? If that's the case, Roger Clemens has been done a great injustice. His anger will be justified. He will have been vilified for no reason. If that's the case, our entire society has been done a great injustice. But if he is in fact guilty, he will no doubt move right to the head of the class that nobody wants to be part of. Let's be fair, but let's be diligent and let's be firm. Our society and our athletes need some tough love.

"Let's get the debate over," says Don Hooton. "There needs to be more Marion Joneses, either in prison, or under house arrest. Get our children on notice that this behavior is not going to be tolerated. It doesn't matter whether it sells tickets or not."

This is where our society needs to be careful. Not every success story in sports needs to be questioned. Sometimes there are just outstanding young athletes who, through hard work and dedication, raise the bar to a new, exciting—and acceptable and legal—level.

There are numerous outstanding young athletes doing just that right now. One is a first baseman for the Philadelphia Phillies named Ryan Howard. He's six-foot-four, weighs about 260 pounds, and can hit a baseball into the next area code. In 2006 he was selected National League Rookie of the Year and Most Valuable Player. He smacked a club record 58 home runs and drove in 149 while hitting .313. But already the whispers have begun. Some make comments that he must be "on something" to hit a baseball that far. This hardworking player—who has done nothing except play the game the way it is supposed to be played—has our cynical sports base wondering if he's on the level. Roger Clemens put himself in situations where his honesty deserved to be questioned. To wonder about Ryan Howard, or any other player who comes onto the scene, is not only wrong, but obscene. Young players deserve the chance to live up to their potential. The increased levels of testing in baseball and other sports will catch the rotten apples who seek to use performance-enhancing substances.

"It's understandable how people might ask about a player like Howard, but completely the wrong conclusion to draw," says author

Lance Williams. "Anybody having a good year is now suddenly suspect. But I don't roll that way. It's not fair and it's not right."

To his credit, Howard has opened up and spoken out about the subject. He's human, too, and he can't help but be affected by such whispers. And remember—he is not the only talented athlete who has to endure the baseless rumors.

"People are entitled to their opinions," he told Paul Hagen of the *Philadelphia Daily News*. "But it does bother me. It casts a shadow on the game.

"I know I'm not using steroids. This barrel right here [pointing to his stomach] is proof enough. People are going to say what they want to say. I thought about it once and then it was like, 'Well, whatever.' I'm not doing it. If they want to test me, they can test me.

"I just think it sucks. The thing about it is, if you're going to make those kinds of comments, have proof. Otherwise, you can ruin people's reputations."

As has been discussed throughout this book, there are different levels of cheating in our society. Some are acceptable, and others aren't. Certainly, the drug culture in sports has changed as society has changed. Our laws and law enforcement officials have dictated that performance-enhancing drugs are an unacceptable step over the line. How that has changed from the summer of thunder with Mark McGwire and Sammy Sosa.

Pitchers will still scuff baseballs, hockey goalies will wear illegal equipment, and high schools and colleges will still occasionally turn the heat way up in the visitors' locker room. And by comparison, such behavior seems pretty innocent. It's all part of the games—an innocent part of games we all have played as kids. Those who compete will always try to get a little edge, a small advantage.

Because of the more serious revelations that have come to light over the past decade, and the scary, potentially tragic willingness of high school kids to try to make their athletic dreams come true by using steroids, we must be even more vigilant.

But equally important is the idea that people are innocent until proven guilty. Hopefully, our society will not take the easy way out and jump to conclusions, prejudging athletes who have done nothing wrong. Success in sports is like success in life. Most of the time, success is earned and deserved because of hard work, honest preparation, and dedication to the craft. But because we're human, we all try to get a little advantage when we can. It is important to remember that we must be even more diligent in protecting the rights and reputations of those who honestly succeed in life as we are in trying to unearth those who ignore the rules of fair play.

It's important to remember, however, that at the end of the day, in the big scheme of things, very few of us actually cross that line between right and wrong—between cheating and just getting a little edge. We're all basically pretty honest, good people. It just seems like the bad ones get all the press.

SOURCES

BOOKS AND ARTICLES

Asinof, Eliot. *Eight Men Out: The Black Sox and the 1919 World Series.* New York: Henry Holt, 1963.

Baker, Earl E. "Stealing Signs Is Cheating. Who Knew?" O.C. Domer, September 12, 2007. http://ocdomer.blogspot.com/2007/09/stealing-signals-is-cheating-who-knew.html.

Bouton, Jim. *Ball Four.* Briarcliff Manor, NY: Stein and Day, 1970.

Casway, Jerrold. *Ed Delahanty in the Emerald Age of Baseball.* Notre Dame, IN: University of Notre Dame Press, 2004.

Cicotello, David, and Angelo J. Louisa. *Forbes Field: Essays and Memories of the Pirates' Historic Ballpark, 1909–1971.* Jefferson, NC: McFarland, 2007.

Davis, Phyllis. *E2: Using the Power of Ethics and Etiquette in American Business.* Newburgh, NY: Entrepreneur Press, 2003.

Douskey, Franz. "Smokey Joe Wood's Last Interview." In *The National Pastime: A Review of Baseball History,* edited by James Charlton. Lincoln: University of Nebraska Press, 2007.

Einstein, Charles. *The Second Fireside Book of Baseball.* New York: Simon & Schuster, 1958.

Engber, Daniel. "The Growth Hormone Myth: What Athletes, Fans, and the Sports Media Don't Understand about HGH." *Slate,* March 24, 2007. www.slate.com/id/2162473.

Fainaru-Wada, Mark, and Lance Williams. *Game of Shadows.* New York: Gotham Books, 2006.

Farrell, James T. *My Baseball Diary.* New York: A.S. Barnes, 1957.

Forde, Pat, and Ivan Maisel. "Stealing Signals, Spying Are Part of College Football Lore." ESPN.com: Cheat Wave, July 2007. http://sports.go.com/espn/2947539.

Hall, Stephen. "Scandals and Controversies." In *Total Baseball*, 3rd ed., edited by John Thorn and Pete Palmer. New York: HarperCollins, 1993.

Hanson, Kirk O. "Culture Suggests Cheaters Do Prosper." Santa Clara University, Markkula Center For Applied Ethics, 2007. www.scu.edu/ethics/publications/ethicalperpectives/culture-of-cheating.html.

Jackson, Shoeless Joe, as told to Furman Bisher. "This Is the Truth." *Sport*, October 1949.

Kalb, Elliott. *The 25 Greatest Sports Conspiracy Theories of All Time*. New York: Skyhorse Publishing, 2007.

Mandel, Stewart. "Breaking the Rules: College Football." *Sports Illustrated*, July 25, 2007. http://sportsillustrated.cnn.com/2007/writers/stewart_mandel/07/06/cheating.cfb/index.html.

Moldea, Dan E. *Interference*. New York: William Morrow, 1989.

Morris, Peter. *A Game of Inches: The Game on the Field*. Chicago, IL: Ivan R. Dee, 2006.

Verrengia, Joseph B. "Ancient Olympics Had Its Own Scandals. Cheating, Gambling Not New to Modern Games." MSNBC.com, July 2004. www.msnbc.com/id/5467740.

Yesalis, Charles, and Michael Bahrke. "Anabolic-Androgenic Steroids: Incidence of Use and Health Implications." *President's Council on Physical Fitness and Sports Research Digest 5*, no. 5 (March 2005).

Zimniuch, Fran. *Going, Going, Gone: The Art of the Trade in Major League Baseball*. Lanham, MD: Taylor Trade, 2008.

———. *Richie Ashburn Remembered*. Champaign, IL: Sports Publishing, 2004.

———. *Shortened Seasons: The Untimely Deaths of Major League Baseball's Stars and Journeymen*. Lanham, MD: Taylor Trade, 2007.

Zumsteg, Derek. *The Cheater's Guide to Baseball*. New York: Houghton Mifflin, 2007.

WEB SITES

Baseball-Reference.com: Major League Baseball Statistics and History, www.baseball-reference.com.

Major League Baseball, www.mlb.com.

National Basketball Association, www.nba.com.

National Football League, www.nfl.com.

O.C. Domer, http://ocdomer.blogspot.com.

Taylor Hooton Foundation, www.taylorhooton.org.

Wikipedia, http://en.wikipedia.org.

INDEX